Parenting Kids with ADHD

Managing Your Child's Explosive Behavior Through Peaceful Methods, Improving Emotional Control & Self-Regulation To Nurture Their Developing Mind to Live a Fulfilling Life!

Natalie Morgan

Copyright © 2023 by Natalie Morgan

All rights reserved.

No portion of this book may be reproduced in any form without written permission from the publisher or author, except as permitted by U.S. copyright law.

Table of Contents

Introduction 8

Chapter 1: Mindfully Managing Your Child's ADHD 12
What Is ADHD? 12
Can We Rule it Out? 13
The Benefits of Evaluation 14
EXERCISE: Emphasize the Positive! 15
EXERCISE: Evaluating the Impact of Your Child's ADHD 16
What is Mindfulness? 18
EXERCISE: Mindful Eating 19
Mindful Parenting and ADHD: Beginning the Journey 21
Action Plan: Mindfully Managing ADHD in Children 22

Chapter 2: ADHD and Executive Function 23
Executive Function and ADHD 23
ADHD and Brain Management Control 25
EXERCISES: Reframing the Parental View of Executive Function 26
The Challenge of Task Completion 28
Mindfulness and Stress 29
EXERCISE: Using S.T.O.P. 29
EXERCISE: Awareness of Breath 30
Informal Mindfulness 30
EXERCISE: Daily Informal Mindfulness 31
Action Plan: Bringing Awareness to Your Child's ADHD 31

Chapter 3: Why Your Self-Care is Important to Your Child 33
The Impact of ADHD On Parents 33
EXERCISE: Give Yourself a Break 34
Taking Baby Steps Toward Change 35
EXERCISE: Decluttering 36
Attention Matters: Do You Also Have ADHD? 37

EXERCISE: Compile a Behavioral Triage List 38
Self-Care Can Help You Get Unstuck From Stress 39
EXERCISE: Paying Attention to Your Stress 39
Make Time For Self-Care 40
EXERCISE: Focus On the Joy in Life 40
Action Plan: Caring for the Caregiver 41

Chapter 4: Change Begins With You 42

Reframing Difficult Experiences 42
The Dangers of Compounding Difficult Experiences 43
EXERCISE: Separating Experiences 43
Seizing the Reins 44
EXERCISE: Fifteen Breaths 45
Fostering Independence and The Executive Function Toolkit 45
Perfection is a Thief of Happiness 47
EXERCISE: Watch the Weather 48
The Rippling Effect of ADHD 49
EXERCISE: Reframe the Parental View On Academic Challenges 50
Action Plan: Externalize 51

Chapter 5: Communication and Mindfulness for ADHD 52

How ADHD Impacts Communication 52
Finding the Middle Ground 53
EXERCISE: Tally Talking Time 53
Actions vs Words: Helping Your Child Repair Communication Flaws 54
EXERCISE: Celebrate Communication Success 55
Mindfulness and Communication 56
EXERCISE: Imagine Communicating Advice to Friends 57
EXERCISE: What's Your Communication Style? 57
Action Plan: Practice Mindful Communication 58

Chapter 6: Using Targeted Praise and Rewards for Success 60

Behavioral Training & Reward Systems 60
EXERCISE: Keep a Gratitude Journal 61
EXERCISE: Establishing a Reward System 62
Using Mindfulness in Praise & Rewards 63
Cut Yourself Some Slack 64
EXERCISE: Give Yourself a Much-Needed Break 64
Action Plan: Focus on Positives in Behavioural Planning 65

Chapter 7: How to Handle Difficult Behaviors 66

Building a Foundation and Creating Boundaries 67
How to Modify Behavior: Time-Outs 69
Grocery Store Meltdowns: What To Do 69
EXERCISE: Ground Yourself 70
EXERCISE: Mindfully Setting Boundaries 72
The Wings That Make Mindfulness 72
Action Plan: Ways To Address a Future Behavioral Crisis 73

Chapter 8: Education and ADHD 74

Executive Function, School Performance, and Policy 74
Create an Educational Plan and Influence the System 75
Keep Mindfulness in Mind 76
EXERCISE: Mindfully Moving 77
Action Plan: Assist With Your Child's Academic Success 78

Chapter 9: ADHD Medication Options 79

Medication Facts and Myths 80
Pros and Cons of Medication 81
EXERCISE: Mindfully Making Decisions 82
EXERCISE: Employing Loving-Kindness 83
Action Plan: Make Treatment Decisions that Benefit Your Child 84

Conclusion 85

References 87

Introduction

"Why fit in when you were born to stand out?"
- Dr. Seuss

Welcome to Parenting Kids With ADHD In order to maximize the benefits of this book it is recommended to acquire the Workbook in this series.

In a society where differences are seen as a bad thing, everyday life can be difficult for children with Attention Deficit Hyperactivity Disorder (ADHD) and the parents raising them. When parenting children with ADHD, there are certain struggles that neurologically typical children may never have to deal with. These struggles can include epic meltdowns, unnecessary arguing, and the appearance of not listening. All of these struggles can make a parent feel like they're running in circles and making no progress.

Many times, parents may feel like they're losing their mind trying to make their young child with ADHD listen to them without fully understanding that the child may simply not fully understand or comprehend what is being asked of them. Children with ADHD are known to be impulsive, struggle with their school work, and have difficulty settling down. As a result, many parents when under stress may resort to yelling, feeling like they're giving in too often for just a moment of peace and quiet, and have trouble staying calm in the face of their child's impulsive behavior. ADHD is known to increase familial stress, which will only make parenting a child with ADHD harder. This can create a cycle of anxiety and worry without peace and harmony in the family home. It's not just the family life that gets disrupted by ADHD, either. This attention disorder is the culprit for many social skill mishaps, communication mistakes, failure to follow through on morning and bedtime routines, poor eating habits, planning issues, and technology use or abuse. Many children with ADHD may have an especially difficult time when it's time to transition from one of the activities that they enjoy the most in order to do something they may not want to do as much, something that often causes outbursts and intense tantrums.

The presence of ADHD in a child can create patterns of unpredictability and unproductivity in caretakers and make parents feel weary and worn down quickly. This also creates another cycle, as this stress will inevitably impact the child and make them feel as if they are the culprit for all the stress and burden they are experiencing at home. No parent wants their child–especially one struggling with ADHD–to feel like a burden or stressor.

But there is hope. These maddening feelings and cycles are precisely why adopting mindfulness in parenting is essential to raising children with ADHD. In this book, you will not only learn what it means to have ADHD and how your child sees the world, but also how to speak to them on a level they will understand. All children are smart, but some need a little help understanding things their way. This may mean presenting instructions or giving commands in ways that are more beneficial, useful, and loving.

This book will assist you with the journey to understanding your child with ADHD and give you powerful parenting exercises that will have you and your child communicating in a healthier way, despite your child's age and your stress. The types of skills discussed in this book are that of practicing focus and attention, as well as personal awareness. Children with ADHD tend to operate on an auto-pilot mode, where they may not be entirely aware of themselves or the impact they have on a situation. By practicing awareness, children with ADHD and their parents can find solace and rationale in the consequences of actions.

This book is designed to assist with understanding mindfulness, its benefits, and its approach to ADHD symptoms. From there, we will discuss ADHD in length and detail, expanding on how ADHD interacts with the brain and how children with ADHD see the world around them. Each chapter will be filled with information and exercises on how to understand your child and how to quell the epic meltdowns that may occur from a child's impulsive nature. We will discuss self-care and why it is so important to parents raising a child with ADHD, so you'll know how you can properly care for yourself and show your child how to take care of themselves, as well.

Developing a new relationship with your situation, your child, and your mindful parenting style may be difficult, but the benefits are entirely worth the time and energy. By using all the exercises within this book and compatible workbook, you and your child will be able to communicate better and more clearly without all the yelling and flushed-face anger that only makes you more angry and your child more sad. As such, one of the biggest factors discussed in this book is proper discipline for a child with ADHD and how to handle the most challenging of behaviors.

Being mindful doesn't mean constant meditation. Mindfulness is more about fostering focus, flexibility, and peace for the whole family. Mindfulness means stopping during a stressful situation, accepting the present moment, and understanding how that moment is making you feel without feeling like you're about to lose your mind.

Parenting children is a difficult and rewarding journey, and raising children with ADHD can feel like a constant battle. The good news is that it does not have to feel that way. By employing all the methods and exercises included in this book to keep calm and open up an honest dialogue with your child, you and your family can break the cycles of stress, anxiety, and yelling.

Familial peace is at your fingertips. Continue reading to begin your journey to mindful parenting.

Mindfully Managing Your Child's ADHD

Beginning the journey to manage your child's ADHD through mindful parenting can feel daunting at first, but the benefits of it can be incredible. First, however, we must look to understand the benefits of evaluating your child for ADHD and what ADHD really entails. From there, we will discuss mindfulness and how this approach to parenting can help you and your family deal with the struggles and challenges that may come with raising a child with ADHD. Throughout this chapter, there will be exercises to help you and your family incorporate this approach into daily life. These exercises will help you and your child focus on the positives of life instead of amplifying the negatives as well as evaluating how impactful the symptoms of ADHD are for the whole family.

What Is ADHD?

ADHD is the acronym for Attention Deficit Hyperactivity Disorder, and it is one of the most common childhood disorders. This neurological disorder is reported by ADDitude magazine to affect between five and eleven percent of all American children (Williams). However prevalent, the symptoms can range from slight to severe. Many of the symptoms include a lack of attention, frequently forgetting what was just said, increased impulsivity, constant fidgeting, hyperactivity, frequent talking (more than a typical child), and trouble with patience. A big factor noticed by parents with their children who have ADHD is a difficulty in following instructions. Sometimes, children with ADHD–especially the younger children between three and five–can have epic meltdowns and tantrums that can leave parents feeling incredibly frustrated.

In order to understand whether or not your child truly has ADHD, we must first take a look at what ADHD is, what the symptoms look like in children, and what it means for your child to live with ADHD. Julie Rawe, from Understood.com, discusses how a child's brain with ADHD differs from that of a neurologically typical child: a large-scale MRI study funded by the National Institutes of Health "shows that some parts of the brain tend to be a little smaller and/or take longer to mature in kids with ADHD" (Rawe). Simply put, the brain in a child with ADHD needs a little longer to mature than that of a neurologically typical child. The brain's relationship to ADHD in children will be discussed in more detail in Chapter Two.

Keath Lowe from VeryWellMind.com discusses what ADHD is like for children: "Children may experience a broad spectrum of emotions, including frustration, feeling lost, disconnection, confusion, overwhelm, restlessness, [and] feeling out of control." Lowe continues by explaining that children with ADHD frequently get labeled as being bad, lazy, or dumb children, which could not be further from the truth.

Can We Rule it Out?

Some children can be very active and hyper without having ADHD at all. In fact, "there is no single test to diagnose ADHD" (Diagnosing

ADHD, n.d.). Instead, there is a comprehensive evaluation that children undergo to make a diagnosis and rule out other disorders. This evaluation is also important for determining co-existing conditions, such as Oppositional Defiance Disorder, for example. An evaluation of this caliber requires time and energy, as well as a detailed medical and family history. This kind of evaluation and diagnosis is made by psychologists, clinical social workers, neurologists, psychiatrists, pediatricians, and nurse practitioners.

The process of ruling out ADHD–or diagnosing a child with ADHD–is a rigorous one that includes biological and psychological considerations. In fact, many other mental health and neurological issues, like anxiety, depression, and some types of learning disabilities can often present with similar symptoms as ADHD. In special cases, such as Autsim Spectrum Disorder, another cause may be a primary diagnosis while comorbid with ADHD as a secondary diagnosis. During the evaluation, a thorough history will be examined from both parents and teachers of the child, as well as the child themselves, when necessary. The first step for diagnosing ADHD is to rule out any other underlying medical issues that could be causing the ADHD-like symptoms. Sometimes, these are the culprits and neurological intervention may not be necessary. In the cases that medical intervention and an evaluation are necessary, there are several mental health professionals that can help. The benefits of undergoing an evaluation cannot be overstated. In the next section, we will discuss these benefits.

The Benefits of Evaluation

Children with ADHD often begin exhibiting symptoms as young as age four. It's about this time they get evaluated for ADHD, but most of the time, children are usually in kindergarten or first grade by the time they see a neurologist. Many times, parents will wait until the symptoms become disruptive to schooling and home life before they seek input from a medical professional. Every evaluation is different and every child is unique. Thus, a diagnosis for ADHD can mean different things for each child. For starters, it's important to remember that an accurate diagnosis is what guides families toward effective treatments. Without knowing what a child is dealing with, a parent may not be employing the best strategies and treatments. In fact, many people can be afflicted from deep sadness and depressive symptoms because their ADHD is not being taken care of in a way that addresses the root causes and they don't see any long-lasting solutions to their challenges.

By evaluating your child for ADHD, you and your child will have a headstart and a team of medical professionals who can decide whether or not medication, therapy, or other forms of treatment are necessary.

EXERCISE: Emphasize the Positive!

Now that we know how important it is to have an evaluation for a child exhibiting symptoms of ADHD, it's time to focus on the positives. Having a child with any kind of disorder– even that of an attention disorder– can be overwhelming and scary. Many parents walk into the neurologists office scared out of their minds that their child will need medication that will take their personality away and leave them a shell of their former self. Most of the time, this simply doesn't happen. In fact, a study published in 2015 by the British Medical Journal, showed that the most common drug prescribed for ADHD improved symptoms and general behavior in children. The study showed that the drug's side-effects included only non-serious adverse effects which included a loss of appetite and trouble sleeping.

That being said, it's important to focus on all the positives in life and the situation as opposed to circling all the negatives associated with your child's diagnosis and future.

Instead of focusing on all the negatives, you may want to employ using positive affirmations to emphasize all the positives of your child's care and well-being. Here are several examples of positive affirmations to employ:

- My child is safe, healthy, and cared for.
- My child's ADHD is part of who they are.
- My child has access to great medical care.
- My child may not need medication.
- Our family may be able to rely on behavioral therapy to solve challenges.

By focusing only on the good things and not on the "what-if" scenarios involving your child's diagnosis, you and your family can rest a little easier and take each event and moment as it comes.

EXERCISE: Evaluating the Impact of Your Child's ADHD

This exercise is all about setting aside some time and really thinking about your child's behavior and their ADHD. Since the evaluation and diagnosis parts are over, it's time to think about how your child's ADHD affects their life, your life, and your family. Sometimes, raising a child with ADHD can come with some extra struggles that can take a whole family by storm. What may have begun as normal child-like behavior may start to feel like it's out of control or happening too often. Children with ADHD often have trouble with the following symptoms:

- Easily distracted
- Not truly listening
- Difficulty paying attention

- Easily forgetting what was said
- Difficulty following instructions
- Requiring constant reminders
- Poor school performance
- Disorganized nature
- Constant climbing, jumping, or roughhousing during quiet playtime
- Constant fidgeting and inability to sit still
- Rushing through things and trouble with patience
- Making careless mistakes
- Constantly on-the-go
- Difficulty with controlling interruptions
- Blurting things out
- Not thinking about their actions, or the consequences of their actions
- Doing things they shouldn't, even when they know they shouldn't
- Trouble controlling emotions, losing their temper quickly, and lacking self-control or self-soothing abilities

Using the above list, take some time to write down all the ways your child's ADHD affects your family. Perhaps your child has trouble with emotional regulation and requires a lot of soothing that leaves you drained. Knowing that this is a consistent issue will aid you in figuring out how to help your child self-soothe and become more emotionally intelligent so that they can better control their emotions in the future.

Try to think of all the effects you possibly can, as this can only arm you with more knowledge to help yourself and your child manage the impact of their ADHD in the home and in your relationship with your child.

Also remember that it's okay to feel frustrated and stressed. Many parents tend to first view their child's outbursts and symptoms as tantrums and misbehavior. While this can leave a lot of parents confused and feeling disrespected, there is hope for both yourself and your child. Learning about what root behaviors are the biggest issues that your child deals with most often can help alleviate some of the tension and anxiety in the home.

What is Mindfulness?

The word mindfulness is tossed around a lot in the modern age of social media, but what does it really mean? In short, "mindfulness is the basic human ability to be fully present, aware of where we are and what we're doing, and not overly reactive or overwhelmed by what's going on around us" ("What Is Mindfulness?" n.d.). The idea behind mindfulness is to still the mind and be present in the current moment. While it's incredibly easy for the mind to wander and for you to be filled with anxiety and apprehension about the future, mindfulness attempts to keep you grounded in the current moment and remind you that there is little need to focus on anything else at that time.

When practicing mindfulness, it's entirely reasonable that your mind may drift off to worry about something, but by focusing on the current moment–on how your body feels seated, or how your legs are moving, or how your breathing is coming in and out–you can remain worry-free and focused on the present. The benefit of adopting mindfulness into your life is that it can help with being overly reactive about situations that stress you out. Instead of getting angry and stressed when the toilet gets clogged, mindfulness can help you accept the current moment and instead of getting overwhelmed, look for a solution (i.e. a plunger).

Some examples of mindfulness include: moving meditation which means paying careful attention to how your muscles, limbs, and body move while you walk, sit, or stand; short pauses in which you focus on breathing or an object; and combining meditation techniques like mindfulness alongside yoga or walking. In truth, mindfulness can be practiced anywhere.

Mindfulness is also known to reduce stress, improve work performance, help you gain awareness of yourself, and allow you to observe what happens in your mind as challenges come your way ("What is Mindfulness?" n.d.).

It's also important to note that mindfulness is not an obscure thing that requires extra purchases or overt change. It's simply the ability to think, "stop," and allow yourself to be present in the current moment. We know that "meditation begins and ends in the body. It involves taking the time to pay attention to where we are and what's going on, and that starts with being aware of our body…" ("What is Mindfulness?" n.d.). You may want to think of yourself floating in the clouds or the ocean and see how it calms your heart rate and removes you from external stressors.

Now that you know what mindfulness is and its purpose, you may now want to practice it in a real-life scenario. In the next section, you'll practice mindful eating, a technique that can help alleviate overeating and disordered eating.

EXERCISE: Mindful Eating

Mindful eating is a great technique for those who are prone to eating too much, too fast. When we eat mindlessly, we tend to eat past the point at which we're full and may accidentally ignore some of the body's signals, eat to quell intense emotions and multitask while eating which will only make us unaware of when we're truly full. Instead, it's important to practice mindfulness while eating, even though some people may find it boring. To get started, you'll get your meal and find a quiet, distraction-free environment. Then, follow these steps:

1. Look at the plate of food in front of you, taking in how it looks, smells, and presents.

2. Take small bites, chewing slowly and not rushing the meal. Take time to savor the dish and truly understand the taste of each component in the dish.

3. Eat in silence, focusing only on the plate of food in front of you, on the way it may sound, look, and taste between bites.

4. Focus on the feelings you get both mentally and physically while eating. This is important to understand when you are done eating or if you need more food.

5. The moment at which you realize you are content, it's time to stop eating and set the food aside. Take a moment to note how much food is left on the plate and how much food you've eaten. This can be used as a guideline in the future to understand how much you truly need to feel satiated.

6. Ask yourself the purpose for which you are eating. Are you hungry? Are you bored? Are you eating simply because the food is tasty or healthy?

You can practice this exercise as often as desired, although one meal per day can suffice for many people beginning their mindfulness journey. By engaging in this mindfulness exercise, you can become more comfortable with the concept of being immersed in the moment and enjoying the present, as opposed to worrying over the past and future.

Mindful Parenting and ADHD: Beginning the Journey

Although the journey may be challenging, being mindful in the face of your child's ADHD-related tantrums and unpleasantries can help you stay calm and react appropriately to impulsive and difficult behavior. Mindfulness is a practice that's been around for centuries, stemming from religions like Hinduism and Buddhism (Selva, 2021). From there, mindfulness was popularized in the East and West, becoming a tool that is often used to remain calm under the pressures of life.

In regards to managing ADHD in a child, mindfulness is used to refrain from screaming, yelling, or getting overly reactive with your child. Unfortunately, managing a child's ADHD meltdowns can cause an incredible amount of stress that can compound into very explosive reactions from parents. Instead, by pausing in the moment and taking a deep breath, you'll better understand and accept what is happening without resorting to screaming and losing your mind. Mindfulness means pausing to accept what is happening in the current moment and focusing on keeping yourself calm. Many times, parents are guided toward bringing attention to their breathing as a way to remain grounded. This means taking the present moment to focus only on breathing and trying to push out every other external factor from your mind. This can be done with nearly anything. While focusing on breathing is a good choice, some parents may want to focus on their bracelet and the colors of it. Some parents may prefer to focus on the feeling of their feet on the floor.

At this moment, so what if your child is throwing themselves on the floor? This moment is meant to help you, the parent, gather yourself and calm your own heart rate and stress levels down so that you can then help your child manage their ADHD symptoms without your own compounding stress. What this does is create a healthier and more resilient environment for the whole family.

This will take much time and practice, but with some work and effort, mindfulness can be achieved and implemented smoothly into your parenting plan.

Action Plan: Mindfully Managing ADHD in Children

Now that you know all about ADHD and mindfulness, it's time to make a plan so as to implement your mindful parenting strategy into everyday life. You won't truly know what works until you've started implementing things, but having a rough draft action plan outlined will help you walk into tantrums a little easier.

Consider making a list of different things to bring your focus to during one of your child's meltdowns or tantrums. By having a few different options, you can experiment with them and figure out what works best for you. You may want to consider implementing two or three different methods in tandem, such as breathing while focusing on a poster.

From there, it's time to put it into action. When a meltdown or tantrum comes your way, use the mindfulness technique to bring your focus to the present moment and try to ground yourself to peace and calmness. When you feel ready and grounded, come back to the moment and focus on what your child is saying, and help them calm down and soothe themselves.

Being a mindful parent can be difficult in the beginning, and the journey is likely not to go smoothly at first. As time passes and you practice more and more, you will find that mindfulness is the best technique for quelling the intensity that can come with ADHD.

ADHD and Executive Function

Executive function is a phrase that may scare some parents because it can sound incredibly formal and daunting. However, it's simply a cognitive skill that enables humans to plan, organize, prioritize, and complete tasks. In children with ADHD, executive function presents differently and leads to struggles with analyzing, planning, and scheduling. Tasks–especially those on a deadline–can be incredibly difficult for children with ADHD. In children with ADHD, this ability is not absent, but has more difficulty following through, and is called executive dysfunction (Barkley, 2021).

Executive Function and ADHD

The phrase executive function was conceived by Karl Pribram in the 1970s, when research showed that these functions were managed by the prefrontal cortex. In children with ADHD, the typical path in the brain that certain questions would take simply isn't followed (Barkley, 2021). There are different circuits in the brain responsible for different types of jobs: what, when, why, and who. In a brain with ADHD, these signals may not make it to their destination and thus cause trouble for a child with ADHD.

The "what" brain signal goes from the frontal lobe toward the back of the brain toward the area where "working memory" is stored. This is directly connected with plans, goals, and the future.

The "when" brain signal goes from the prefrontal area of the brain toward the cerebellum at the back of the head. This signal is all about timing and behavior, punctuality, and when we do certain things. This explains why some children with ADHD may struggle with time management.

The "why" brain signal is the third circuit and comes from the frontal lobe toward the central part of the brain. This is linked with emotions, control of emotions, and emotional intelligence. This is the signal that chooses among multiple options and makes decisions. Without this signal being delivered, tantrums and emotional meltdowns can be common and expected. For a child with ADHD, they may simply not understand their emotions because the brain signal is not following its path to completion.

The final brain circuit is the "who" signal and goes from the frontal lobe to the back of the hemisphere, where self-awareness is located. This is where we are aware of what we do, how we feel, and what is happening to ourselves. A child with ADHD may lack self-awareness and not realize the impact of their actions due to this signal being absent.

It's also important to note that executive function is important to seven specific social skills: self-awareness, inhibition, non-verbal memory, verbal memory, emotional regulation, motivation, and problem solving (Barkley, 2021). Any parent of a child with ADHD already knows that these seven areas of life can be incredibly difficult for their child.

ADHD and Brain Management Control

Now that we know more about executive function and the role it plays in ADHD in children, we can discuss the brain management and control functions of a child with ADHD. In a study published in The Lancet and financed by the National Institute of Health, 3,000 children and adults were examined using MRI brain scans ("Large-Scale MRI Study," 2017). Slightly more than half of the participants have ADHD. The findings of this research give greater insight into how the brain of a child with ADHD differs from that of a child without ADHD:

- Five of seven areas of the brain were smaller in children with ADHD.

- The region of the brain with the greatest size discrepancy was the amygdala, the area that is most related with emotional and self-control. This area also specializes in the ability to prioritize tasks.

- Regions of the brain linked with learning and memory were also smaller.

- Medications for ADHD are not the culprit for the size discrepancies. Children who are medicated for ADHD exhibited the same size differences in the same areas as those who never used medication.

- In adults with ADHD, the size discrepancies did not exist. It appears that the size becomes similar between those with ADHD and those without after the teen years.

You may be wondering what these findings mean for you, as a parent. Well, there are a few things we can do with this information.

First, it proves that ADHD is a real brain condition with physical and presentable evidence ("Large-Scale MRI Study," 2017). This, in itself, can be incredibly calming and validating to know that this is not something "made up."

Second, while the brain scans show that children will grow and their brains will get to the appropriate size in the five regions where it may be small, ADHD symptoms will not go away ("Large-Scale MRI Study," 2017). As a lifelong condition, ADHD may require lifelong intervention, therapies, and strategies to assist in treatment.

Third, this study proves that children with ADHD may simply not understand their full range of emotional intelligence or their ability for self-control until they reach a more mature age. This is not to be discouraging, but instead motivational. This is a thread of hope; continue to work with your child on emotional intelligence and self-control. Eventually, they will grasp the concepts well.

EXERCISES: Reframing the Parental View of Executive Function

Because parenting is already an arduous task, it can be incredibly upsetting to know that there is something going on in your child's brain that you can't quite fix, not that children with ADHD are something to be fixed. However, it can feel that way during times of high stress.

Instead of wallowing helplessly, it is integral to your mindfulness and parenting journeys to reframe the way in which you view Executive Function, your child's ADHD, and the stigma of ADHD. Children with ADHD may already start to wonder what's wrong with them, so getting ahead of these thoughts is ideal. There are two sure-fire ways to reframe your parental view of executive function and ADHD: positive affirmations and structure.

Positive affirmations are essentially a goldmine of positivity. They are something that parents of children with ADHD are in desperate need of. Some of the best positive affirmations are those that bring you to the present moment. These affirmations are a piece of mindfulness and will help assuage those worries and fears that creep in when your thoughts begin to ruminate. Consider making your own affirmations or using some of the following:

- "There is nothing inherently wrong with my child. They have flaws like the rest of us, but they are kind, loving, and good."
- "My child's ADHD does not define them."
- "My child requires my love, patience, and assistance."
- "I am going to model good emotional intelligence for my child by refusing to yell at them for their outbursts."
- "My child is constantly learning, even when they are having a difficult time controlling themselves."
- "ADHD is my beautiful child's superpower!"

Take some time to write your own affirmations, specific to your children and your ADHD experiences. Remember to try and reframe the experience positively, such as, "My child needs a good role model for expressing appropriate emotions," as opposed to, "My child is screaming and I'm going crazy." Reframing the experience into what your child needs works wonders.

The second surefire way to reframe your parental view of ADHD and executive functions is to provide a consistent structure for your child. Children with ADHD typically require more structure than children who do not have ADHD (Orenstein, 2010). A child with ADHD will be more amicable to changing tasks and going throughout their day when they know what to expect and when to expect it. It may not need to be a very strict schedule or followed all the time, but it certainly should be implemented for daily use. Having a routine or structure will help a child with ADHD accept the day ahead with fewer epic meltdowns, especially if there is a small warning ahead of time to let them know the progression of the day.

Take some time to create a routine to help you and your family establish an expectation for your child. Go over the routine with them so they know what is expected of them. Ideally, a routine for the morning (before school, perhaps) and a routine for bedtime are the best ways to ensure quiet and smoother transitions between activities. However, the beginning will be difficult. It may take your child a few days to get the hang of it and patience will serve you well during this time.

The Challenge of Task Completion

I remember asking my daughter to take a bath five times one afternoon after school only to find her on the floor with her dolls after two hours of my asking. She was quietly fabricating stories with her toys, her clean clothes piled beside her as she played, as if she'd simply gotten side-tracked. Which is exactly what happened. For children with ADHD, focusing, retaining attention, and keeping information are difficult and contribute to the failure to complete a task ("How to Help Your Child," n.d.).

The solution is a touch simple: break the task into a few smaller tasks. Instead of asking my daughter to take a bath after that first mishap, I'd instead ask her to gather her clothes, a much smaller and more easily completed task. Then, I'd ask her to turn the water on. When completed, I'd ask her to gather the toys she'd want to play with in the tub. Finally, when the clothes were gathered, the toys were collected, and the tub was filling, I'd ask her to take a bath. Usually, this was done without fuss or fight.

Try this method yourself and see how small the steps are that your child requires in order to maintain the instruction and follow through with the complete task.

Mindfulness and Stress

Now that we have discussed ADHD at length and you're now equipped with several strategies to specifically handle your child's ADHD, let's talk about you. Raising your child and handling your child's ADHD might be causing an insurmountable level of stress to build on your shoulders. Using mindfulness, you can keep that stress in check and keep it from pummeling you into the ground.

An archaic method of meditation, mindfulness has been studied by some of the top universities in the world and found to provide assistance with building emotional strength and resilience toward external stressors (Alidina, 2019). Mindfulness means pausing to tap into your own mind and avoid reacting to a situation until you have yourself together. Mindfulness can help you be more in tune with your thoughts, aid in reactions to stress, bring awareness to your needs, bring awareness to your emotions, and foster feelings of compassion inside yourself (Alidina, 2019).

Let's discuss how to quell stress using two mindfulness techniques that are ultimately tried and true: using S.T.O.P. and bringing awareness to your breath.

EXERCISE: Using S.T.O.P.

S.T.O.P. is an acronym and one of the best mindfulness techniques out there. This is meant for those really intense moments when your child is having an intense meltdown and you simply aren't sure what to do. You might be on the verge of screaming, but it's integral to model emotional intelligence and keep your cool. Using this technique can help you create some mental room for you to ease your worried mind before you tackle the issue (Goldstein, 2013). The acronym means the following:

- Stop

- Take a breath
- Observe
- Proceed

The core principle is to pause and keep from reacting. You'll respond to the external stimuli after you have breathed and observed what is happening in front of you. By using this technique, you'll be able to remain present and handle outbursts with the utmost grace.

EXERCISE: Awareness of Breath

In a similar vein to S.T.O.P., awareness of the breath is simply the act of pausing for a set amount of time and breathing. It's all about being in the present moment and paying attention to every detail of the air filling your lungs and leaving your lungs.

Get into a comfortable position, ideally in a quiet environment, and focus on being in the moment. Focus on the way the air moves through your body and be mindful of the thoughts coming in and going out of your head.

Do this for any amount of time you'd like; five minutes is the recommended start time.

Informal Mindfulness

Busy parents, never fear; mindfulness is a technique that can be done during the busiest of days. This is called informal mindfulness. Karen Pace from Michigan State University discusses the differences between formal and informal meditation, saying, "...practices can also be adapted into informal practice...When we practice mindfulness in a more informal way, we are noticing our experience from moment to moment and bringing out attention to one thing as many times as we can throughout the day" (Pace, 2016). This means something as mundane as washing dishes can be a mindfulness exercise if we take time to feel how the soap feels against our skin and how the water feels on our hands. It also means slowing the movements down to truly appreciate every moment of the feeling.

EXERCISE: Daily Informal Mindfulness

There are dozens of ways to implement informal mindfulness into daily life. Here are several:

- *Walking*. Take careful note of how your body moves when you walk, how your hips, legs, and arms feel.
- *Sitting outside*. Watch nature around you, feel the warmth of the sun on your skin, and notice how the wind feels through your hair.
- *Showering*. Take note of how the soap feels on your body, and how the water feels going over you.
- *Driving*. Carefully pay attention to what you see, how the steering wheel feels in your hands, and the sounds of driving around you.
- *Breathing*. Awareness of the breath can be done anytime, anywhere, even in a crowded place.

Action Plan: Bringing Awareness to Your Child's ADHD

In this chapter, you have learned a lot about ADHD and mindfulness. You have learned several strategies and techniques on how to carefully and mindfully take care of yourself and your child. You have also learned more about executive function and how to reframe ADHD in your parental viewpoint.

Now, it's time to look ahead. You have a wealth of knowledge about ADHD and how it affects a child; it's time to take that knowledge and spread it. To someone who doesn't know much about ADHD, your child may come across as hyper, unteachable, and incapable of listening. You know better. You know there is a real reason and that your child is completely normal. It's time to spread that knowledge.

By bringing your child's teachers, grandparents, and siblings up to speed on ADHD and how it affects their loved one, you and your support system can work as a team to help your child get the care, patience, and emotional resilience they need. It may not be easy, but you have the mindfulness techniques and strategies to help implement systems to help. Get out there and make sure everyone knows how they can help you as you help your child.

Why Your Self-Care is Important to Your Child

Raising a child with ADHD is hard. Not a single person can contest that claim. This is why it's so important to take care of yourself. You cannot possibly take care of your child if you cannot first take care of yourself. Think about being on an airplane while the flight attendant is discussing what to do in an emergency. The advice is to always put your mask on before putting one on your child. This is because you are important for your child's safety. You must be there to take care of them, emotionally and physically. That being said, let's get into the impact of ADHD on parents and marriage, and strategies on how to conduct self-care when raising a child with ADHD.

The Impact of ADHD On Parents

In a study conducted by Dr. V A Harpin at the Ryegate Children's Centre in the United Kingdom, it was discovered that ADHD "may affect all aspects of a child's life" (Harpin, n.d.). In fact, the study goes on to say that parents and siblings are at risk for "disturbances to family and marital functioning" (Harpin, n.d.).

As a child grows, the symptoms of ADHD change and evolve. The aspects of the disorder vary and continue into adulthood with other types of troubles in occupational and personal life.

Parents may have a particularly difficult time finding childcare for young children with ADHD as some family members may not want to care for the child. Parents may also feel discouraged by their child's difficult time in social situations and any difficulties finding friends. Poor sleep patterns with children who have ADHD are common, as well, and can cause an incredibly difficult time for parents who are not getting enough rest as a result (Harpin, n.d.). Additionally, Harpin suggests that parents raising a child with ADHD may struggle to find time to themselves and thus may have strained family relationships, particularly in a marriage (Harpin, n.d.). He also mentions that parents of sixty-six children with ADHD expressed more dissatisfaction in their parenting journey than those of children in a control group (Harpin, n.d.).

Simply put, parenting a child with ADHD is difficult and is associated with a higher level of stress, less sleep, and more difficulty in dealing with emotional outbursts and tantrums.

EXERCISE: Give Yourself a Break

Because of all the aforementioned troubles that can come with raising a child with ADHD, it's incredibly important to take care of yourself as needed. It's not only for the sake of modeling good self-care habits; sometimes you simply need a moment to yourself.

I'll never forget one night when I was exhausted and basically a zombie. My daughter just couldn't sleep and the extra energy inside her was keeping us both awake. My partner came to me and ushered me into our bedroom. "Do you want control or peace?" he asked me. At the time, it didn't make much sense, but then it dawned on me. I needed to give up the control I was trying to exert by begging my child to simply sleep and accept the break my partner offered me.

It is important to give yourself a break and accept the help as needed. You are a parent, not a machine. Even if you need a five-minute breather alone in the bathroom, take it. You deserve a break– or five– throughout the day!

Taking Baby Steps Toward Change

You and your family aren't going to be able to make leaps and bounds in one night with any of the goals and changes you wish to make. Instead, it's going to take persistence, time, and patience. In the previous chapter, we discussed employing mindfulness techniques in daily life as well as setting up a structure for your child. Now, we will discuss the need to employ self-care methods throughout the entire journey of raising your child with ADHD. As with all parenting, there will be easy days and there will be hard days. The point of self-care is to build resilience and make yourself more capable of handling difficult times when they arise.

It can be easy to forgo self-care for the sake of your children, but making the change from no-self-care to decent-self-care is vital to your mental health and well-being, not to mention your parenting methods.

Starting the journey to self-care is rife with little steps to take every single day. There are a number of small steps that you can take each day to improve your self-care routine and find time to rebuild your emotional resilience. Here are a few ideas:

- *Taking naps or getting to sleep a little earlier.* I know, sleeping is the antithesis to fun–even as an adult–but sleep is vital to your emotional resilience and your ability to mindfully parent.
- *Exercise daily.* Some parents may actually find exercise incredibly invigorating and beneficial. For others, it may feel

more like a chore.

- *Eat healthy foods.* Relying on junk food will only make you feel like junk while eating healthy food can boost emotional resilience.

- *Get outside.* A walk through nature can help reorient someone who has ruminating thoughts, and vitamin D from the sun can help keep depression and anxiety at bay (Scaccia, 2020).

- *Spend time with a pet.* Pets have the ability to boost happiness and offer emotional support to many people.

These are only a few of the small self-care things that can help build emotional resilience. Others can include going out for drinks with friends, engaging in a favorite hobby, or relaxing with a good book.

EXERCISE: Decluttering

One of the best ways to remain mindful is simply to have less to worry about within the home. With less, you aren't worried about the mess, the clutter, or the stress associated with constantly cleaning. When the area around you feels too messy and cluttered, you may experience difficulty figuring out how to center yourself (Greiner, 2020). Mindfulness can also be practiced while decluttering, as it will bring your mind to the present moment and focus your energy so that you feel like breathing is easier.

While decluttering may not sound like a pinnacle of mindfulness or parenting for ADHD, it does offer a reprieve from daily stress in small doses. When that kitchen counter is clean, making meals is easier, which can make all the difference during the day.

While decluttering, practice mindfulness by taking a good, slow look at everything you are attempting to declutter. Examine the items with your eyes, with your hands, and with your other senses. Feel the weight of each item as you place it where it belongs in the home. Bring yourself to the present moment and focus on the task at hand without letting your mind wander to other things, like worries, stresses, and anxieties.

Attention Matters: Do You Also Have ADHD?

While modern medicine isn't exactly aware of the factors that contribute to ADHD, it has come up with a few components that may work together to be responsible. One of those components is a genetic factor. ADHD can run in the family line ("Attention Deficit Hyperactivity Disorder," 2018). Research has indicated that both parents and siblings of a child who has been diagnosed with ADHD do commonly have the disorder themselves. The disorder is complicated, however, and there are other factors at play.

That being said, it's entirely possible that a member of the family may have passed the condition down the line to your child. You and your partner may wish to evaluate yourselves to get more answers and insights into your family. This would also be beneficial for your child as they grow into adulthood.

We've discussed the symptoms of ADHD in children, but we haven't touched on the symptoms in adults. The following list is a compilation of symptoms that some professionals believe are exhibited in adults with ADHD ("Attention Deficit Hyperactivity Disorder," 2018):

- Inattention or nonchalance.
- Picking up new projects without finishing old projects.
- Underdeveloped organizational skills.
- Difficulty with focus and identifying priorities.
- Constantly misplacing things.
- Frequent forgetfulness.

- Trouble with interrupting or remaining quiet for long periods of time. Also, trouble with impulse control when speaking.

- Varying mood swings or an inability to emotionally regulate.

- Difficulty handling stressful situations.

- Intense impatience.

- Engaging in risky activities with little regard for safety measures, such as speeding when driving a car ("Attention Deficit Hyperactivity Disorder," 2018).

If you have noticed your child's ADHD, it's time to look within and see if you exhibit any of the symptoms of ADHD in adults. If this is the case, you may want to pursue medication or therapy treatments to help deal with the disorder. Knowledge is always the first step in creating change. Knowing about your own struggles is also a form of self-care itself, as you will now be armed with the necessary information that will pave the way in helping you take better care of yourself and your mental health.

EXERCISE: Compile a Behavioral Triage List

Think about your behavior. Do you show any symptoms of ADHD? What types of symptoms do you see in yourself that may coincide with this disorder? It's time to write each of these symptoms down in a bulleted list and examine each one.

Next, you'll take some time going through each symptom, and you'll decide how to best handle your own behaviors. For example, if you feel you're too forgetful, you may want to start carrying around a planner or small notepad to write down important dates and appointments. If you feel that you interrupt too much and get distracted mid-conversation, you'll probably want to remove any potential distractions from the area while having an important conversation.

Write down each symptom and a corresponding solution that you can refer to in a pinch. By doing so, you'll be helping manage your own ADHD symptoms, model good coping strategies for your child with ADHD, and taking care of yourself by giving yourself the attention you deserve to build a better you.

Self-Care Can Help You Get Unstuck From Stress

Self-care in itself is a form of attention. It's just one that you're giving much needed attention to yourself. Stress can come in many forms and can plague you with worries and woes of a future that has not even happened yet. Pausing and using mindfulness techniques while taking care of yourself can help you get unstuck from the constant pit of anxiety and worry that can drag you down. This means that taking fifteen deep breaths while taking a bath can boost calmness and reduce stress. This is a form of self-care and attention.

Mindfulness is a form of focus and attention that seeks to accept the current moment without judgment or fear, which can ease stress and tension ("Focus More to Ease Stress," 2011). Consider combining self-care techniques with mindfulness to bring attention to your stress and expel it from your day.

EXERCISE: Paying Attention to Your Stress

It might seem counterintuitive to focus on your stress, but it can be incredibly helpful. Bringing your attention to the issue at hand—whether a tense traffic jam or a problem at work—can help you realize the true weight of the situation. Think about the issue and then imagine it as a helium-filled balloon floating away into the air and popping into the atmosphere.

There is no reason to worry about what you can't change. Let the issue float away from you and then use a mindfulness technique to bring your attention to something else entirely.

Make Time For Self-Care

Waiting for some time to magically appear in front of you for some downtime will only leave you disappointed. Chances are that time isn't going to come. You'll have to schedule time in your day to allow for self-care. After all, being the last thing on the long list of daily to-do's doesn't feel good; although, you may not realize that if you aren't adequately paying yourself enough attention ("Why You Need to Make Time for Self-Care," n.d.).

By scheduling it, you'll be making yourself a priority and modeling good self-care skills for your children. Without appropriate self-care methods, you may run the risk of "burnout, depression, anxiety, resentment, and a whole host of other negative implications" (Glowiak, 2020).

Instead of waiting, take your planner out and write a chunk of time to dedicate just for you. Or perhaps pull up your digital calendar and allot a time slot dedicated to your own personal care. Whatever method you choose is perfect if it gets you the self-care you need.

EXERCISE: Focus On the Joy in Life

It can be easy to fall into a pit of despair and focus only on the negative, but this will get you nowhere and will only make your mind a sad and dark place. Instead, engage in some positive affirmations about life that will invoke positivity, love, and hope. Here are a few examples:

- "I deserve to take care of myself and shower myself with nice things."
- "I deserve to be happy and experience calm moments."
- "I adore my child's laugh."
- "I appreciate the fresh air in my lungs and the quiet environment around me."

- "I am excited for the vibrant future ahead of me."

Action Plan: Caring for the Caregiver

Now that you know how important it is to give yourself time, attention, and care, it's time to make yourself a priority in your action plan. Remember that you are integral to the proper functioning of your family unit and fundamental in your child's ADHD experience. Taking care of yourself means that you can take care of your family. That being said, think about the best ways that you can implement self-care into your day. Is there a specific time of the day that is most ideal? Perhaps a walk or a gym session after your child gets on the bus is the best thing for you. Maybe, you'd rather take a long and luxurious bath with your favorite book after the kids are in bed. Anything that makes you feel refreshed, alive, and ready to handle any stress thrown your way is perfect.

Now, schedule your self-care time each week or more as needed, and you'll start to see an improvement in your emotional resilience in no time.

Change Begins With You

As the parent of a child with ADHD, you are the ultimate role model. You will be the one to show your child how to express their emotions and how to expand their knowledge of emotional intelligence and resilience. You may feel like it's too hard sometimes to be your child's ultimate source of knowledge about the world. This is why it is so vital to your parenting journey that you make small changes to your own operation in order to provide your child with the proper foundations for their own adult life. In this chapter, we will discuss how to reframe certain viewpoints and offer exercises on how to adopt mindful practices and thought processes that will help your child thrive.

Reframing Difficult Experiences

A technique called cognitive reframing can help ease some of the frustration you may feel during your parenting journey. "Cognitive reframing is a technique used to shift your mindset so you're able to look at a situation, person, or relationship from a slightly different perspective" (Morin, 2021). When a negative experience happens in life, it can be easy to get caught in a loop of negative thoughts and emotions. It may feel good to ruminate on the issue instead of solving it, but this is not good for anyone. Instead, you'll want to shift your viewpoint so that you are able to see the reality of the situation without your bias.

Reframing your thoughts may be hard, but it simply boils down to how that situation has a silver lining. Instead of thinking about how exhausting it is to handle some of your child's outbursts, you may instead want to view them as learning experiences for your child. When looked at through a lens of positivity, difficult experiences can morph into powerful lessons as opposed to hard realities.

The Dangers of Compounding Difficult Experiences

Each event is its own experience, in its own bubble of information that should not be compounded with other events. This means that, as a parent, you must manage each huddle as its own unique event without judgment, bias, or prejudice. Maybe your child has spilled juice on the floor for the eighth time this week, but by compounding all eight experiences into one big, messy ball, you'll only feel rising irritation and get yourself worked into a frenzy about the cleaning process.

Instead, it's important to separate and isolate each frustrating experience so that they don't build up into an emotional tower that will eventually collapse from the stress. This may be difficult for some, but try the following mindfulness technique to help the events fizzle away from you and avoid letting that emotional tower build up.

EXERCISE: Separating Experiences

Sit with your legs crossed, wherever is the most comfortable place for you. Close your eyes and imagine each irritating experience as if it were a bubble. The bubble can begin at your face and begin floating upward until finally it pops and the little particles of it drop to the floor while the air inside goes up toward the sky.

Imagine the air inside of the bubble is the frustrating experience you've had. Let it go up and dissipate into the atmosphere away from you. Let it leave you in peace and harmony as you remain grounded. By imagining this, you can let go of the experience and separate yourself from the frustration. Do this with each individual experience, being sure not to compound them. When you are done, slowly open your eyes, take a deep breath, and continue your day with a calmer mindset.

Seizing the Reins

Making little changes is all about a sense of control. No one else can cause little changes in your life besides yourself. You have the power to build the life, family, and world you wish to live in. By employing the small methods outlined in this chapter, you're one step closer to taking the reins of your life and directing your world instead of following the path laid out for you. Remember that you are in control of your life even if you can't control every aspect of life or other people in your life (Williamson, 2021). Use the following affirmations to remind yourself that you are in control of your life and motivate you:

- "I choose the best path for me."
- "I may not be able to control everything, but I control how I respond and react to things."
- "I am learning new ways to change and adapt every day."
- "I can breathe through challenges and emotions without losing my cool."
- "I deserve to build a world I'm proud to live in."

EXERCISE: Fifteen Breaths

Mindful breathing is a great way to build up emotional flexibility and reduce the effects of stress and anger ("Mindful Breathing," n.d.). This exercise is done by focusing on the way the air enters and exits your lungs for fifteen consecutive breaths. During particularly stressful moments, you may want to take a larger breath in for three seconds, hold that breath for two seconds, and exhale through the mouth for four seconds ("Mindful Breathing," n.d.). If you are not feeling overly stressed, you may want to simply examine each breath as it comes into you and leaves you, focusing all your attention away from the current stressor.

Fostering Independence and The Executive Function Toolkit

Cultivating independence can be a difficult job for a parent. The desire for independence begins rather young in children. At around first and second grade, children desire to choose their own clothing, walk home from the bus stop alone, or go to bed at a later time (Anthony, n.d.). Some changes will be appreciated by you but others might make you feel like you're going to rip your hair out. Some of the decisions your child wants to make will have you tugging at your hair in frustration and make you extra cautious as you watch your child venture through life.

Around the age of seven, children can think more abstractly and make rational judgments. They also learn more about the value of pros and cons, actions, and causes and effects, which are all skills integral to fostering independence (Anthony, n.d.). As previously mentioned, a lot of these abstract concepts, like emotional regulation and self-control, are difficult for children with ADHD to cultivate. At around age seven, these skills develop across the board and executive functions may begin to improve remarkably.

Another note to add by an author for Scholastic, Michaelle Anthony, is that the U.S. Department of Education states that children have peak performance when they have strong parental connections while expressing differing viewpoints (Anthony, n.d.). Parents are vital to the independence of a child and a cornerstone to fall back on when emotions run high.

All of this information on independence is fundamental to the toolkit you will want to create for the improvement of executive functioning in your child with ADHD. This toolkit will be beneficial for a child as young as four–the age at which symptoms begin to arise–and can be used throughout the entirety of adolescence. It can also be modified as needed. Because some of the main issues for children with ADHD are working memory, emotional regulation, and task completion, the toolkit includes the following:

- *Coping activities for outbursts and emotional turmoil.* Many children may find it difficult to keep themselves under control when they have ADHD and intense emotions. By first validating and accepting those emotions, children can then move on to distracting themselves from the pain with a separate activity.

- *Practicing gratitude and positive affirmations.* By practicing gratitude with your child, you can make them more aware of the good things in their life to focus on, as opposed to the negative. Positive affirmations can boost their self-esteem and quell the concerns they may have about their condition.

- *Giving your child choices throughout the day.* Letting your child pick out their school clothes, their snack, or which video game they want to play during their allotted screen time can be a great way to quell outbursts and make them feel like they have a say in what happens to them. It will also make them feel like they have control over their lives and their body.

- *Encourage your child to ask for help.* A child with ADHD may find it difficult to get tasks done and then get incredibly frustrated at any roadblocks in their path. Allow them the space to try things on their own but also encourage them to ask for a helping hand when necessary.

Perfection is a Thief of Happiness

Striving to be the perfect parent and raise the perfect children will only set you up for incredible and heartbreaking disappointment. Not only will being a perfectionist stress you out but it will be harmful to the well-being of your child. A perfectionist mindset–and the stress and anxiety that comes with it–is not something you would want modeled for your child, so it is integral to refrain from modeling this type of behavior. Instead, you will want to find a good middle ground in which your child can thrive;one where they are not burdened by the need for things to be perfect and know when they need to rest.

There are many signs that signal you are expecting too much from yourself as a parent (Morin, 2021). These include:

- Frequent criticisms of yourself.
- Placing blame on yourself when your child does something wrong.
- Comparing your parenting journey to others and feeling like you don't meet the standard.
- Constantly beating yourself up for not doing more with or for your child, regardless of how much you do.
- Second-guessing your choices as a parent.
- Resorting to yelling or screaming as a result of your impossible-to-meet standards.
- There are also many signs that indicate your expectations for

your child are too high and that you are seeking perfection from them (Morin, 2021). These include:

- Having a hard time observing your child do something incorrectly.

- Constant micromanaging as your child works on something.

- Pressuring your child to perform without flaw.

- Encouraging your child to pursue your dreams, not their own.

- Placing all your self-esteem and self-worth on your child's success.

- Viewing your child's normal activities as if they are life-altering experiences.

Children, and parents, for that matter, cannot thrive in an environment where the standards are unattainable. It's time to let go of perfection and let things go as they may. Next, we will discuss an exercise to help ease the perfectionism burden and allow you to simply exist in the present moment.

EXERCISE: Watch the Weather

In this exercise, you'll want to grab a drink of your choice and take a seat near a window or outside, wherever comfortable. A seat on the porch, in the house within view of the outside world, or on the lawn are preferable. Ideally, you'll want to be able to feel the sun on your skin. Next, you'll simply bring your focus to the weather outside, watching as the cloud cover interrupts the sunshine or how the rain sounds as each drop hits the concrete sidewalk outside. The idea during this time is to bring your attention specifically to the weather and avoid letting your mind wander. If it wanders, you might get swept away in a sea of emotions or anxiety. Remember: anxiety is the act of living in a future that hasn't happened yet. This exercise seeks to avoid getting lost in the cycle of living in the future that hasn't happened yet, the millions of "what-if" scenarios, and the fear of the unknown.

Spend fifteen minutes simply watching the weather and try to observe things you may never have noticed before while keeping your focus on the present. This exercise is ideal for people who enjoy the sunshine or the rain, both of which can be calming.

The Rippling Effect of ADHD

Researcher Judith Wiener discusses the ripple effect of ADHD in her study published by Sage Journals: "Adolescents with attention-deficit/hyperactivity disorder (ADHD) are highly vulnerable. Although their hyperactive symptoms tend to decrease from childhood through adolescence, their inattentive symptoms remain stable. Their academic, social, and emotion regulation difficulties persist and they are at risk for co-occurring oppositional defiant disorder, conduct disorder, anxiety, and depressive disorders" (2020). The effects of ADHD, essentially, ripple throughout the child's entire life and support system. Wiener mentions that self-perception and relationships inside and outside the home are of particular risk for the rippling effect. Trouble with academic and behavioral issues is not dismissed from the argument.

While this may sound like a bad thing, it's not entirely terrible news when a child knows how to manage their ADHD symptoms. The key to handling this rippling effect is love, attention, and fulfilling the emotional and mental needs a child may have. This means having less pressure placed on them to be perfect and understanding their emotions, actions, and consequences for behavior.

EXERCISE: Reframe the Parental View On Academic Challenges

Many parents may have a difficult time letting go of the need for their child to be a perfect student, but this is entirely unnecessary. Academics may play a large role in your child's life, but the mental and emotional well-being of a child is much more important than their academic performance. The stress and emotional exhaustion of getting perfect grades can be almost too much for a child with ADHD ("Emotional Health," n.d.).

Thus, it's time to use positive affirmations to reframe the way that you may view your child's grades and the priority you place on their academic achievement. These affirmations should focus on the positive side or silver lining of a situation. Here are a few examples of silver linings and positive affirmations you may want to adopt:

- "My child's health matters more than their academic performance. If they are exhausted, they need rest first."

- "I can help my child find a way to understand the material better through online or tutoring resources."

- "My words, attitude, and actions impact my child more than I know; I have the power to encourage them to be positive and take it slow when they need to" ("Emotional Health," n.d.).

Keep in mind that a child with ADHD may have a harder time focusing and will stumble through a lot of their academic life. This is not uncommon or unusual and will require a lot of patience from you, the parent. However difficult, it is possible for your child to succeed in academics, although it may not be the way you envisioned it.

Have patience with your child and remember to keep your focus on the positive to reframe your view.

Action Plan: Externalize

Now that we realize that a lot of small pieces of the puzzle begin with you, you can move on to making sure that all the little stressors in life don't remain locked up inside your chest and foster negativity.

Instead, engage in the fifteen breaths and watch the weather exercises to release the negative experiences and let them drift away from you. Start each new day from scratch, knowing that it will never be a carbon copy of the one before it. Use breathing, mindfulness, and reframing techniques to reassure yourself that things don't have to build and bubble up inside you and that you can instead let go of negative mindsets. By doing so, you will build a healthier and happier environment in which your child can thrive, regardless of their ADHD diagnosis.

Communication and Mindfulness for ADHD

When raising a child with ADHD, you may find yourself repeating your words much more often than you want, or feel like you need to. This is incredibly common when communicating with children who have ADHD. While it may be frustrating and difficult to manage, communication can be fostered in healthy ways using behavioral training, positive rewards, and open dialogue. In this chapter, we will discuss the science behind ADHD and communication, as well as offer techniques on how to foster mindfulness in your parenting style in regard to your child's communication trouble.

How ADHD Impacts Communication

The underlying issue with communication and ADHD is that ADHD "represents a deficit in executive function, a skill set that includes attention, impulse control…and far more. [ADHD is] seen as a disorder of self-regulation" (Bertin, 2014). Thus, children with ADHD may experience language delays in early childhood and suffer from frequent distractibility, interrupting, and trouble with listening to "rapidly-spoken language" (Bertin, 2014).

This doesn't mean that your child is without hope! Using behavioral training methods, even children as young as four can experience growth and development in their communication skills. This is not to say that your child will be a master communicator within a year from the beginning of therapy; the change will be slow, but incredibly beneficial as children grow and develop using positive habits.

Finding the Middle Ground

Having a conversation with another person is typically an exchange in which two people listen and speak in an alternating pattern. When it comes to holding a conversation with a child with ADHD, alternating patterns do not exist. It can be difficult for them to wait their turn to speak and they often get distracted by other thoughts. The middle ground between complete conversational chaos and control lies with redirection. When your child goes on a tangent a touch too long, it's okay to gently reel them back into the topic at hand.

For example, if you and your child are having a conversation about puppies and your child goes on a branching tangent conversation, you can simply say, *"Let's finish this conversation before we start a new one."* You may even want to add, *"There's more about puppies that I want to say. Is it okay if we finish this topic first and then you can choose the next topic?"* This has a three-fold benefit of reeling your child back into the conversation, giving them a measure of control by allowing them to pick the next topic, and modeling better communication habits for them to use in the future.

EXERCISE: Tally Talking Time

An effective strategy for helping a child with ADHD and communication trouble help reorient their conversational technique is to allow them to speak and tally up the exchanges you and your child have. This means that every time your child speaks, they get a tally, and every time you speak, you get a tally. At the end of the conversation, you both will compare the tally marks together to make sure there is an equal amount. If the tallies are particularly uneven, in favor of your child's side, you can discuss with them that it's important to listen to other people and hear others' thoughts as well as express their own.

Using tally marks, you can help your child understand their impact on a conversation and how important it is to hear other perspectives.

Actions vs Words: Helping Your Child Repair Communication Flaws

All development requires action. Research from The University of Waterloo in Canada has shown that children with ADHD may have a much harder time to consider other perspectives compared to children without ADHD ("Studies Link ADHD," n.d.). This study showed that ADHD and communication issues are directly linked and that children with ADHD struggle to understand another person's viewpoint during a conversation.

Therefore, discussing different perspectives and trying to understand the world outside your child's own viewpoint may not click with them. Instead, you'll want to take action. Here are some practices you and your family can take to help your child understand other viewpoints:

- When your child states you are not listening to them, pause. Take time to listen to them speak and let them know that you have stopped, listened, and understand their perspective. De-escalate the situation by letting them know you hear them. This is not to change your mind on the conversation, but to model the idea that you–and they–can accept that other perspectives exist.

- Make a chart. Some children with ADHD learn better with hands-on activities or with visual aids. A chart depicting a staircase, ladder, or sidewalk can illustrate the steps in a conversation and the different stages of communicating.

- Make a rhyme out of it. Children as young as three can learn rhymes and commit them to memory. A rhyme might be just the thing to make your child remember that they must be kind and consider other perspectives.

- Practice asking how your child feels; then, ask your child to inquire about your feelings. This can help your child get into the habit of seeing how other people feel and take those feelings into consideration.

EXERCISE: Celebrate Communication Success

When your child has done something particularly wonderful and surprising regarding their ADHD symptoms, you must celebrate their success. This will incentivize future communication changes. The more you celebrate your child's success, the more they will strive for the parental approval you give them. Here are some appropriate and healthy ways to celebrate your child's success:

- Take them out for ice cream.

- Go outside and play catch with them.

- Play their favorite video game with them.

- Instill a material reward system, in which they can choose an item from a box of physical toys, stickers, or trinkets.

- Allow them extra screen time on their favorite game, app, or show.

Ideally, whenever your child shows success and achievement in a conversation, you will want to reward them accordingly. You won't, however, want to give them too big of a reward for minor achievements, as they may get too used to how easy it is to gain a reward and might reduce the effort they put in.

Also, make sure you are giving them high-fives, hugs, and positive words of love and affirmation. Affection is crucial for a child, and children with ADHD tend to feel unloved, unwanted, and excluded due to some of the behavior they exhibit. Parental affection can go a long way in reducing these emotions and making them feel loved and supported while they adjust their behaviors.

Mindfulness and Communication

Mindfulness is about pausing and paying attention to the present and current moment. By doing so, you can identify personal traits that you want to grow within yourself and habits you'd like to expel. Regarding communication, mindfulness means having awareness and handling responses appropriately. This means moving out of autopilot and taking control of yourself before responding. This can be difficult in a heated conversation or debate, but it is an infinitely better solution than resorting to screaming and yelling. By pausing to understand your own reactions, you'll be better able to understand why you feel this way. There could be a multide of reasons you reacted in the way you did; whether you simply woke up cranky, are focusing too much on the past, or find yourself lost in your thoughts. To have a mindful conversation, you'll want to have awareness of your thoughts, emotions, physical sensations, and your body language (Bertin, 2016). Bring yourself an understanding of these aspects of your body before you continue the conversation.

When you bring yourself awareness of what is truly happening inside you, you can handle a conversation with your child in a more measured and productive way.

EXERCISE: Imagine Communicating Advice to Friends

One of the best exercises to do when struggling with one of your problems is to imagine what you would say to your friend if they were having this issue. Sometimes we can be too hard on ourselves and set our expectations too high.

Instead, pull yourself out of the situation and imagine one of your friends telling you how they are suffering with this issue. Likely, the advice you administer during this imaginary conversation is what you believe you should do.

Trust yourself and listen to the advice you give without any bias that comes from within.

EXERCISE: What's Your Communication Style?

It is integral to know what your communication style is and how that affects the way you and your child with ADHD communicate together. There are four styles and they operate in starkly different manners:

- *Passive*. This communication style is marked by indifference and constant yielding to others ("4 Types," 2018). If there was a style for doormat, the passive style would be it. The passive types usually do not engage outwardly in communication but instead remain silent and let anger and resentment build inside them. These communicators typically don't make eye contact, have poor posture, and have difficulty saying "no." They also have notoriously poor self-esteem and self-trust.

- *Aggressive*. Aggressive communicators speak in booming and demanding voices while maintaining excessive eye contact. These communicators tend to dominate conversations, projects, and are often controlling. They may also blame, intimidate, and criticize others often. While they can be good leaders and get things done quickly, they can be commanding, rude, and may have trouble listening to others.

- *Passive-Aggressive.* Of all the communication styles, passive-aggressive is the most toxic and uncomfortable. These communicators are passive on the surface but have such intense build ups of emotions that they often spill out in the most inappropriate places. These communicators often gossip about others, mutter under their breath, and use facial expressions that don't link with what they are saying. These types lack open communication and are prone to silent treatments and sabotaging others.

- *Assertive.* Of these four types, assertive is the most beneficial and effective type. In this communication style, a person is able to effectively state what they need, isn't afraid to speak up, and cooperates well with others. These types express their needs, desires, ideas, and feelings while being considerate of others. These communicators have one goal: to have win-win situations in which there is a good balance of good and bad for everyone. Assertiveness strives to take ownership of feelings and behavior without blame and without letting those emotions control their actions.

Action Plan: Practice Mindful Communication

Now that you know how difficult communication can be for your child and their ADHD symptoms, you'll want to set realistic expectations. Your child will not be a master communicator in a few months or years. Instead, this is a lifelong journey toward self-improvement and executive function development. It will take plenty of effort and time.

Remember to employ mindfulness exercises, including S.T.O.P. and fifteen breaths from a previous chapter, as well as tallying up your talking time and giving advice in your head to sort through difficult challenges. By using these methods, you can keep your cool while helping your child develop their communication skills.

Using Targeted Praise and Rewards for Success

In the previous chapter, we discussed using praise and rewards for conversational and behavioral success in communication. In this chapter, we will expand on this idea and discuss how this method can dispel negative behavior while incentivizing the adoption of positive behaviors. By employing these methods, you can show your child that you love them, appreciate them, and want the best for them in life.

Behavioral Training & Reward Systems

A reward and praise approach to handling ADHD is not new; you may have even stumbled across this method in one of countless parenting books. Schools tend to use this method to incentivize positive behaviors, as well. The way behavioral training works is that positive or desired behaviors are rewarded immediately while negative behaviors receive immediate consequences (Low, 2020). Without discouraging negative behaviors, you run the risk of your child falling off track and misremembering the desired behaviors and modifications.

The way this system works is in three easy steps (Low, 2020):

1. *Determine which behaviors should be modified.* In this step, you'll want to specifically name which behaviors you want to eliminate and define target behaviors to replace this negative behavior (Low, 2020). For example, a child who insults other children's art frequently may only be rewarded when they praise another child's art.

2. *Install a system of rewards as a result of good behavior.* In some cases, a tier list may be required here in which the value of the reward is comparable to the value of the action. Little actions may elicit little rewards while bigger actions can elicit bigger rewards. Regardless of the reward, your child must find the reward motivating enough.

3. *Stay with the program. Consistency is key.* It is important for your child to develop the positive habit of the modified behavior. Without a consistent application of the plan, the rewards may have little or no impact and the negative behaviors may not change in the long-term.

Using these three steps, you and your family can find peace, happiness, and modified behavior that empowers your child.

EXERCISE: Keep a Gratitude Journal

This exercise can be done alone or with your child. If you think your child would benefit from naming a few things they are grateful for, you can ask them to do it with you. This mindfulness technique is meant to pull you from stress and anxiety and bring you to the present moment. The idea is simple: think of five things you are grateful for in that moment. These things can be the weather, the air you breathe, the food you eat, your child's laugh, or your relationship with your partner. Try to phrase these gratitudes in a complete sentence that illustrates why you are grateful for that thing or person. For example, instead of writing "I am grateful for my child," consider writing "I am grateful for my child's curiosity and ingenuity." By identifying the specific parts of your child that make you grateful, you can boost your gratitude and overall happiness.

Try writing at least five things to be grateful for every day to boost gratitude and positive thinking.

EXERCISE: Establishing a Reward System

It may take you extra time to establish a reward system that works for your child, as it may be hard to procure rewards, think of rewards that will motivate your child, or make a tier list for different rewards. For example, you may want to assign different positive behaviors with different corresponding rewards. For example, children who don't particularly enjoy washing dishes may be incentivized with larger rewards or more desired rewards. Considering making a tier list like the following (or modify the following to fit your needs):

- Desired Uncommon Behaviors
    - Sharing toys
    - Self-soothing tantrums (and not screaming)
    - Walking away from stressors and fights with siblings
        - Incentives: A trip to the park, baking cookies with mom or dad, a trip to the ice cream parlor or skating rink
- Desired Common Behaviors
    - Doing the dishes
    - Vacuuming the rug

- Putting away laundry
    - Incentives: A whole sticker sheet, fifteen minutes of playtime outside, extra screen time
- Desired Frequent Behaviors
  - Helping a sibling with something
  - Saying kind words to someone
  - Doing something when asked the first time
    - Incentives: A toy, trinket, sticker from the reward box

Remember that while giving the incentive to your child, it is vital to explain to them why they received the incentive and what behavior you expect to see in the future. Also give them a high-five, hug, or kiss on the cheek to show them how much you appreciate their hard work and love them.

Using Mindfulness in Praise & Rewards

Now that we've discussed how praises and rewards work, we can touch on employing mindfulness in the process. Mindfulness, as previously mentioned, is about being present in the current moment. As such, you can employ mindfulness in your praises and reward system by simply shoving everything aside and focusing on the here and now.

Consider taking a deep breath before retrieving the reward box in order to ground yourself in the present moment, and letting your awareness rest solely on the breath in your lungs. When you feel grounded, go ahead and grab the reward options.

Focus on the way your child lights up as they choose a toy from the reward box, observe the way the toys feel in your hand as you shuffle through them, and notice the things that your child is most interested in. Keeping your focus on this moment can help you observe what your child likes the most from the box and what you should replenish the box with, as well.

When your child has picked a toy, focus on the weight of the box, the sounds and words your child says as they walk away with the toy, and how you feel watching your child learn.

When you feel grounded and calm, you can resume your normal activities feeling much more rested and at ease in the present time.

Cut Yourself Some Slack

There will be moments in which you forget to give your child their incentive for a job well-done. There will also be times in which you feel so utterly swamped with work, home, or school stuff that you forget to give your child a high-five. You aren't the only busy parent in the world, and it's entirely reasonable that some rewards will slip through the cracks.

Beating yourself up for missing a reward, falling out of the habit, or forgetting to replenish the reward box will do nothing for you or your child. Instead, cut yourself the slack your deserve and work toward getting back on track. Your energy is better spent getting back to your child's care and behavioral development than beating yourself up. Remember that perfectionism is the thief of happiness. If you've forgotten a reward, praise and affection can substitute in the meantime; give your child a random high-five, hug, or kiss on the head to make sure they know they haven't been forgotten and reassure them that you will always come back for them and their success.

EXERCISE: Give Yourself a Much-Needed Break

Breaks are necessary, especially when attempting to adopt new mindsets and behaviors. You can easily get emotionally and physically drained from the demands of keeping up with behavior training and employing mindfulness throughout the day. When this emotional drainage occurs, it's time to take a step back and let yourself have a break. This may mean asking your parents or partner to take over the behavior training for a day or two while you collect yourself. There's no shame in pausing to take care of yourself. Consider taking a warm bath, reading a nice book, or going out for some much-needed time alone.

Action Plan: Focus on Positives in Behavioural Planning

Behavioral training can be difficult, but by using mindfulness to keep yourself grounded, the battle is already half-won. Make sure that you are giving yourself just as much praise as you are showering your child with. You deserve all the encouragement, just as your child does. Stick to the plan and give yourself a break, as needed.

How to Handle Difficult Behaviors

It is not uncommon for children with ADHD to struggle with emotional maintenance and control. Frequently, children with ADHD tend to have defiant and combative behaviors, which can manifest in a multitude of ways ("Does ADHD Raise the Risk," n.d.). Often, challenging behaviors will include emotional outbursts, the chronic refusal to follow an instruction from a parent or teacher, and distaste for doing things that they know they struggle with. Transitions are particularly hard for children with ADHD, and they may start acting out when asked to do certain things like stop playing, do their school work, or get ready for bed ("Does ADHD Raise the Risk," n.d.).

However difficult, these behaviors can be tamed, modified, and handled in various ways, especially by employing mindfulness and mindful approaches to parenting. We have discussed employing a reward system with your child, which can be a great first step in behavior modification. Next, we will discuss how to further modify behavior by creating boundaries and modifying behaviors that cross over the line.

Building a Foundation and Creating Boundaries

A foundation for behavior expectations is a perfect start to fostering a healthy connection between your child and the world. This means you'll want to show your child what they can reasonably expect from the world around them and how they are expected to act in the world, as well. For example, teaching your child that they cannot have their sister's new birthday toy simply because they want it is a good place to start. Children with ADHD may not understand what the big deal is and why they can't have their sister's toy, but explaining it to them, regardless of their understanding at the current moment, can help them understand later on. The more you give them the explanation, the more they will understand it later. Each time you see your child expressing intense emotions about something unreasonable, you may want to pull them aside and try to explain the limits and boundaries of the situation they are in. You may get frustrated about their seeming lack of understanding, but these explanations will click eventually.

Often, neurologists and medical professionals will suggest that you and your child begin a behavioral therapy regimen to assist with your child's ADHD-related behavioral issues. For preschool aged children, a lot of this therapy is more focused on giving parents the tools and techniques to help handle difficult behaviors that may otherwise drive both parent and child crazy. The two different types of training through these therapy sessions are Parent-Child Interaction Therapy (PCIT) and Parent Management Training (PMT), both of which have a myriad of benefits that can help both parent and child ("Does ADHD Raise the Risk," n.d.). The following list describes the benefits of these therapy methods and how they can help your child manage themselves and help you handle their difficult behaviors:

- Increased awareness of positive child behaviors that can be rewarded, if the family is using a reward system.

- Instilling the idea that minor misbehaviors should be ignored.

- The training necessary to keep consistent with consequences for major behavioral issues or aggressive acts.

- PMT focuses more on helping the parent develop specific skills related to a child's behavior.

- PCIT revolves more around the interaction between child and parent while the therapist acts as a mediator and evaluates which skills to develop for their communication and growth together.

- Both PMT and PCIT have been noted to decrease negative behaviors in children, such as disruptiveness, belligerence, and defiance ("Does ADHD Run the Risk," n.d.).

- Parents who engage in either type of therapy program have indicated a lowered level of stress and improved relationship with their child.

Discussing boundary-setting in these therapy sessions can give you and your family a clearer idea of how to handle challenging behaviors and develop a more personalized approach to your child's care.

One more way to set boundaries with your child is to make clear and precise schedules and routines for them to follow. Discuss these schedules and routines with your child and make sure they understand any rules, such as "no sugar an hour before bed" or "no TV time until your teeth are brushed." Test out the routines for a few days and don't be afraid to modify them, as needed. Sometimes, a routine simply will not work for you and there's nothing wrong with switching it up a little.

As with anything, there can be obstacles to creating your foundation for boundaries and setting these boundaries can be present. Common obstacles with setting boundaries can include not following through or a lack of consistency. These two obstacles are the biggest and often contribute to a backslide in progress. By giving up on the plans you make and not following through–or only following through sometimes–you run the risk of confusing your child and making it hard for them to understand what is expected of them. Steer clear of these two major pitfalls and stick to your plan to make it serve your family well!

How to Modify Behavior: Time-Outs

One of the most tried and true methods of discipline for a child is the classic time-out. This method is one of the most used for younger children. For children with ADHD, a time-out is more than a disciplinary method; it can be considered a method of self-care for your child. Things can get very stressful or over-stimulating for a child with ADHD and by removing them from the situation and placing them in a calmer and more manageable environment, they may be able to calm down faster, easier, and with much greater ease than if they were still exposed to the stressful event, person, or environment. After an episode of undesirable behavior, a time-out should be immediately employed and should last only one minute per age of your child. For example, a seven-year-old would have a seven-minute time-out.

After some repetition, your child will come to understand that this consequence will happen when their behavior is unacceptable and can serve as a reminder to not behave in a particular way.

Grocery Store Meltdowns: What To Do

Sometimes, no matter what you do, you will still have to deal with the classic grocery-store meltdown, especially if your child is under the age of five and has ADHD. While completely expected, it can be incredibly stressful for you, as the parent, to watch your beautiful child pounding their fists on the shelves, throwing something in anger, or kicking their feet on the floor because you won't get them a toy they want.

That being said, the first thing you'll have to do is take a deep breath. Every time you have witnessed a child throwing the same type of tantrum that your own child is throwing, you have likely never passed judgment, made a remark, or thought anything negative (aside from, perhaps, "Thank God, that's not my child"). Remember that no one is judging you, thinking you're a bad parent, or paying much attention to your situation at all, for that matter.

When you've come to terms with this, calmly remove your child from the stressful situation. A trip to the bathroom might help as it can be quieter. Perhaps, you'd rather leave your cart in a place you remember and take your child to the car. This is even more effective if you have a partner available to assist with shopping or discipline.

When your child has been removed from the stressful situation, give them some time to quietly calm down. This may take several minutes for them to fully relax. At that time, explain to them why you removed them from the store and what you expect from them and their behavior. An apology may be required if hurtful words were said by either parent or child. Discuss with your child ways that you both think they can keep from having emotional meltdowns and try using these methods the next time a meltdown occurs. You may, however, have to pull your child out of the grocery store on multiple occasions if they're still under the age of five or six, as they may not fully understand what they are doing wrong.

EXERCISE: Ground Yourself

Grounding yourself is an incredibly important step in making sure that you don't overreact when your child is in the throes of a meltdown. Instead, you'll want to wait until after you've grounded yourself before responding to the stress. This can feel difficult at first, but when you have practiced grounding techniques enough, you'll be able to do it without thinking twice. Here is a list of grounding techniques that will help you respond rather than react to an ADHD-related meltdown:

- *Bring awareness to yourself, your name, your age, and where you are.* By bringing focus to yourself, you can help alleviate the stress you are feeling from your child's behavior.

- *Take fifteen slow and intentional breaths.* Focus your energy on the breath in your lungs and how they feel entering and exiting your body.

- *Drink cold water or wash your face with cold water.* Water is notoriously helpful for bringing the mind to the present moment. The method of consuming water you choose doesn't matter as long as it works to help your heart rate slow and your stress level come down. Some people prefer to rinse their wrists in cool water.

- *Focus on the words on a poster or item.* By reading something, even if it is meaningless to you, you can bring your mind to the present moment and focus on something that isn't the thing bringing stress to your body.

- *Bring your attention to five things you can see, hear, touch, or smell.* If your child is having a meltdown, you may want to go with five things you can smell or see to turn your attention away from the stress you may be feeling from the tantrum. List those five things in your head before bringing yourself back to the issue at hand.

Use these grounding techniques to bring awareness to yourself and remain calm before handling your child's difficult behaviors.

EXERCISE: Mindfully Setting Boundaries

This exercise is all about making a list in a mindful state. You may want to wait until your child is tucked into bed at night to make this list, as you will have more uninterrupted time to mindfully think about which boundaries should be listed.

First, use one or more of the aforementioned grounding techniques until you are in a state of calm and peace. When you are fully aware of your calmness, your breath, and your state of contentment, turn your mental attention to the memories of your child's behavior and the areas in which they have crossed boundaries with you. This could be something like not knocking before opening the door, or something as severe as pushing their sibling during an argument. Write down as many behaviors you can remember and what boundaries they crossed. Things like aggression, violence, and name-calling are common boundaries in a family and a good place to start.

If you start to feel yourself get frustrated with the memories, do another grounding technique to remain calm.

When you have your list, you can work toward creating a defined plan of which behaviors are the highest priority for modification and which behaviors can be ignored. You may also want to create a list of rewards that your child might receive for going a certain amount of time without a meltdown or for expelling a negative behavior for a certain period of time.

The Wings That Make Mindfulness

Cindy Ricardo, from A Caring Counselor blog, discusses that the two wings of mindfulness can be summed up into two concepts: wisdom and compassion (Ricardo, n.d.). If mindfulness were a bird, one wing would include insight, thought, and observation– all things that would make up the concept of wisdom. The other wing would include compassion, intention, relaxation, calmness, and loving-kindness

(Ricardo, n.d.). The idea here is that there is a balance between seeing and observing a situation and looking at that same situation with love and calmness. Ricardo states, "There must be a balance between compassion and wisdom, to help us stay present with the challenges we face in life, and to learn from them" (Ricardo, n.d.).

Looking at your parenting journey for your child with ADHD can require a lot of patience and loving-kindness. You may want to use this metaphor during your child's next meltdown or difficult behavior and first observe their actions before applying a very thick layer of loving-kindness to the way they are feeling. Look at your child's actions by balancing like a bird's wings in the wind by saying: "Yes, I see my child having a temper tantrum, but they are feeling strong emotions and need help getting used to them."

When you change your perspective toward kindness and love, you will see your child coming to you with their needs more often and with greater respect.

Action Plan: Ways To Address a Future Behavioral Crisis

Now that we have discussed challenging behaviors, it's time to formulate a plan to put your new information into practice. Remember to make a list of your child's most disruptive or high-priority behaviors that tend to cross the boundaries in your home. Now, using those behaviors, discuss consequences, schedules, and routines with your child. Clearly, and lovingly, discuss your expectations of them and their behaviors while being realistic that there will be hiccups along the road to developing and modifying behavior.

Laying the foundations for your child's behavior will take time and energy, but these boundaries will serve your child well in the coming years. Don't forget to ground yourself during the process and respond rather than react to their tantrums. Remember: this, too, shall pass.

Education and ADHD

It's no secret that children with ADHD tend to struggle with academic performance a little more than their peers. The symptoms of their disorder tend to make it harder for them to focus, sit still, and control their impulses. This can mean that children with ADHD might interrupt a lot during lessons, fidgeting with their hands and feet, or get up and walk around when they aren't supposed to. There are options to help children with ADHD thrive academically. Much of this help can be from you, their parents.

Executive Function, School Performance, and Policy

As discussed earlier in this book, executive function include several key features in decision-making, including the ability to pay attention, achieve mental flexibility, the ability to control impulses, and "working memory, [which is] a temporary storage system in the brain that holds several facts or thoughts in mind while solving a problem or performing a task" (Low, 2020). As such, school performance can be deeply impacted in children with ADHD since they will have a harder time with some—or all—aspects of executive function.

As a child grows and matures, some of these symptoms may be easier to handle, especially with medication as needed. There may be run-ins with school policies, however, that require sitting still for long periods of time. The best thing to do is discuss your child's ADHD diagnosis with a representative or guidance counselor at the school your child attends. "To meet the needs of children with ADHD, schools can be part of effective treatment plans for children with ADHD; and provide special education services or accommodations" ("ADHD and School Changes," n.d.). This means that a school can participate in your child's special accommodations for attention, whether this means a smaller class, special one-on-one education, or extra materials.

As children approach high school, there may be a higher demand for attention and impulse control. Fidget toys can help, as long as they are quiet. ADDitude Magazine discusses how children can stay focused on classwork:

- Use colored pencils or highlighters to organize notes.
- Review notes as often as possible.
- Quietly multitask during class, if needed. Sometimes, there's nothing wrong with doodling during a lecture.
- Break large tasks into smaller ones. Instead of thinking of it as a five-page essay, think of it as a one-page essay that you have to do five times. This might make it feel more manageable.

Create an Educational Plan and Influence the System

"The best approach considers each child's strengths and vulnerabilities, as well as each individual family's needs and functioning" (Calderon, 2020). With the help of your child's school and your own intuition, your family can create an educational plan that can work well for your child and share that plan with other parents of children with ADHD to help them, too. It may be hard at first, but by using trial and error, as well as helping other parents in your position, you can make the school system more aware of the needs that a child with ADHD has. It's not that these children are troublemakers like they've been made out to be, they simply need more time to understand concepts. Help influence the school system by sharing your experience with your child and sharing the tips that truly work with other parents.

Keep Mindfulness in Mind

Much of the time, you and your family will need to remain patient and calm with your child. Their ADHD symptoms may start to become more manageable but ADHD is a lifelong condition and their inattention, struggle with sitting still, and forgetfulness may never fully disappear. For the rest of your life with your child, you will have to keep in mind that they may have difficulty listening, paying attention, and not "zoning out" in the middle of your conversation. Your child will, however, improve in a myriad of ways. Likely, your child will learn emotional control and be able to battle back the impulses to do things they shouldn't.

When you find yourself frustrated with them as they go through their academic lives, remain calm and don't forget to respond rather than react. Elementary and middle school can be particularly difficult as executive functioning may not have had enough time to be fostered adequately yet. However, "these skills are extremely malleable and amenable to improvement," says Johanna Calderon of Harvard Health (Calderon, 2020). This means that executive functioning in children can be boosted and developed at very early ages. Calderon goes on to suggest that the answer to much of the stress related to your child's ADHD-related executive functioning status is mindfulness: "To tackle both stress reduction and executive function improvement at once, mindfulness training seems like an ideal candidate" (2020). Try practicing mindfulness techniques you've learned in this book with your child and see how their listening skills are much more improved after the technique is over.

Remember the wings of mindfulness we discussed in the last chapter: wisdom and observation. Keep your mind open and watch as your child goes about their academic life, intervening with loving-kindness as they need. Children with ADHD may need more love and reassurance from their parents due to the difficulty they experience in school. The idea isn't to help them ace classes–although they might need assistance with this as well–but instead to make sure they understand that it's okay if they aren't fully understanding everything.

EXERCISE: Mindfully Moving

Try this exercise with your child and see how they respond to the technique. This can help your child–who may have trouble with constant distraction–draw back into the present moment without interruption.

First, begin walking. Then, when you are at a comfortable pace (ideally, a slow pace in an environment that brings you and your child comfort and peace), begin saying "left, right" with each movement of the corresponding leg movement. This means you'll say "left" when your left foot goes forward and "right" when your right foot goes forward. Continue this technique for just a few minutes and observe how being in the present moment affects your child's mood, listening skills, and peace of mind.

While this may feel boring at first, the idea is to bring your child's mind to the current moment and free them of any other thoughts so they can practice their attention skills.

Action Plan: Assist With Your Child's Academic Success

First and foremost, your plan of action for academics with your child is to remember to keep your cool and be mindful. Mindfully think about your child's educational progress and keep yourself in a state of calm. Your child may require more time and attention than other children, may need more help at home with their assignments, and may need more materials or assistance with projects. There's nothing wrong with this, although it can be frustrating when your forgetful child doesn't mention that their model of a cell is due at 9 am the following morning and you've already changed into pajamas, but now you must run to the store.

With time and patience, your mindful parenting skills will foster a healthy and safe connection for you and your child to tackle any academic challenges that may arise. Remember to use all the mindfulness techniques outlined in this book, especially the Mindfully Moving technique, wherein you forgo all other worries and remain as calm as possible while simply focusing on your movements. By doing so, you can release some of the frustration and worry that you may feel about your child's academic performance.

ADHD Medication Options

Medication. The word itself can sound scary. Any parent in their right mind would blanch at the word and think, "Why does my child have to be on medication?" Concern and uncertainty about ADHD medication are normal. Truthfully, your child may not require medication. Ken Ensroth, a medical doctor and psychiatrist for Providence Child and Adolescent Psychiatry, discusses medication treatments for children with ADHD and their side effects. In this chapter, we will discuss his findings; however, he mentions: "Medication can never be a substitute for parental involvement. My best advice is to keep the lines of communication open with [your child], [their] teachers, and other people who are important in [their] life" (n.d.). No matter whether or not your family chooses to use medication for your child's ADHD symptoms, parental patience, love, and attention must always be present.

Medication Facts and Myths

There are a lot of myths about ADHD medication that tend to get circulated and scare worried parents. Some of these myths have zero basis in reality. Here are a few that have been easily expelled by a 2019 blog post from Millenium Medical Associates:

- **Myth #1: ADHD medications are new and untested.** ADHD medications have actually been prescribed without long-term health effects for over 50 years.

- **Myth #2: ADHD medication is unsafe and has terrible side effects.** All medications have some side effects, yes, but the side effects of ADHD medications are not life-threatening or serious.

- **Myth #3: ADHD medications can act as gateway drugs.** Research actually suggests the opposite: ADHD patients who have been adequately treated are less likely to use illicit drugs.

- **Myth #4: You don't need to take your ADHD medication if you're not working or attending school.** Some people might be able to focus better at home than at school or work; for them, maybe this method works. It may not work for every patient. Each patient is advised to follow their doctor's regimen for medication and discuss with their doctor when it may be appropriate to skip a dose.

- **Myth #5: ADHD medication is unnecessary.** Everyone is different; some patients may not be able to function appropriately without ADHD medication. Focus for some ADHD patients can be so difficult and overwhelming that they do require medication.

Pros and Cons of Medication

Most of the time, stimulants are used to help aid or erase the symptoms of ADHD, but they can have different effects on everyone. Sometimes, a doctor may have to try a few in order to find the one that works the best for your child. These stimulants work to "improve concentration, memory and organization by boosting the effectiveness of neurotransmitters, the chemical messengers that carry information throughout the brain" (Ensroth, n.d.). These stimulants typically take effect incredibly fast and patients are likely to see differences in a matter of days.

Benefits of ADHD medication include the following:

- Improved attention
- Decline in hyperactivity
- Reduction in impulsiveness
- Boosted academic performance

Side effects are present with nearly every type of pharmaceutical. The side effects of ADHD medication can include:

- Mild loss of appetite
- Difficulty sleeping
- Frustration or anxiousness

Note, however, that some patients never experience any side effects from their ADHD medication.

Ensroth also mentions that if families are too nervous about medication options, there are other options to consider (Ensroth, n.d.). These options include working with teachers to improve academic performance, teaching your child organizational skills by using planners or agendas, and putting your child in a physically demanding sports or music program, which can help with social interaction and be a good outlet for energy.

EXERCISE: Mindfully Making Decisions

Now that you have learned a little more about medication options for your child's ADHD, it's time to use mindfulness to keep yourself calm while making decisions. Remember the wings of mindfulness that we discussed earlier in this book: wisdom and loving-kindness. Use observation with compassion to decide, mindfully, which option is best for your child.

First, you'll want to sit in a peaceful place. You may want to close your eyes or bird-watch in the park while attempting this exercise. Bring your awareness to your lungs and your breathing. Focus on inhaling, holding your breath for a moment, and feeling the way your breath exits your body. When you feel a sense of calm come over you, think about your child's ADHD symptoms. Simply observe them in your head, remembering the times your child has struggled with forgetfulness, impulse control, or emotional regulation. Try to take your emotions out of the observations you're making in your head and simply accept and understand the behavior.

Next, consider how often your child's symptoms creep up. Are these symptoms a common disruptor in your child's daily life? How often are these symptoms interrupting your child's functioning? Consider if your child would benefit greatly from medication using only compassion as a lens. Think about how much you love your child and want what is best for them.

Some parents may decide that they would like to pursue medication to ease the discomfort their child may be feeling inside their busy minds while others may feel like their child can function at a typical range without medication. After using both wings of mindfulness, which side are you leaning towards?

Repeat this process as needed and discuss the choice with your partner as well. Show them how you thought about the choice to see if they have more insight to add to your situation.

EXERCISE: Employing Loving-Kindness

Loving-kindness is a meditation that we have mentioned in this book a few times. Now, it's time to try it. This exercise is meant to give and receive love from yourself and from others.

First, you'll want to get in the most comfortable position possible. This can be seated, lying down, or however you'd like. Allow yourself to access a deep well of calm and open yourself up to the abstract concept of love. Imagine that you are sitting by a well and inside is a swirl of all the affection and love you hold. Now, you'll practice giving some of that affection you have for other people to yourself.

Ask yourself: What do I need? This may be hard for you to answer, and for some who are not used to caring for themselves, this can feel uncomfortable. Push the discomfort aside as much as you can and focus on the question, letting anything that comes into your mind take root. Perhaps you need more connection, love, or freedom. Whatever you need, write down or take a mental note.

Next, ask yourself: What do I most want to hear from other people? Feel free to write these down as well. Anything that makes you feel the most excited and giddy whenever someone says them to you, write them down and focus on how happy those words make you feel.

Now, you're going to give those words to yourself. For those who needed love or wanted to hear that they are loved, you'll say, "I love myself," or, "I love you," into a mirror. Other common chants or affirmations used during this process include:

- I am worthy of affection.

- May I know emotional peace from my strife.
- I belong.
- May I know that I am the architect of my life.
- I adore my ambition.

Try out any phrase that you think you need to hear and see how they feel. You may discover something about yourself was missing and you didn't even know.

Action Plan: Make Treatment Decisions that Benefit Your Child

As your child's parent, you are the best person out there to decide what option is the best. Consider your child's quality of life in a mindful manner. Consider how they might benefit from ADHD medication. If they're an older child, ask them how they feel about the choice. If your child is younger, you may want to pursue cognitive behavioral therapy before using medication. With any option, there will be positives and negatives. The fact that you are even considering your options for your child's well-being means you are an amazing parent who loves their child and wants their success over everything else.

Bring awareness to yourself and your child and try to think about your options using the wings of mindfulness: compassion and observation. There are likely no wrong choices here.

Conclusion

Mindfully parenting can be a difficult challenge, but the reward is rife with peace, patience, and a thriving relationship with your child. By adopting a mindful parenting approach to ADHD symptoms, you'll be helping your child focus on all the positives in life as opposed to catastrophizing all the negatives.

In this book, you've been armed with all the ADHD information needed to make the best possible decisions for your child's emotional, academic, and medical care. Perhaps, through these words, you have decided that therapeutic intervention would benefit your child, that you'd like to employ a reward system to help with difficult behaviors, or that you'd like to consult with your child's medical team to discuss medication options.

We've spent a great deal discussing research studies and information involving executive function and how incredibly important parental patience will be during a child's formative years, especially when they show symptoms of ADHD. It can be hard to keep your cool under the pressure of grocery store temper tantrums and emotional outbursts, but using the mindfulness techniques explored throughout these chapters, you now know how to best handle these situations.

By stopping before reacting, bringing awareness to your breath, and taking fifteen slow breaths, you'll be ready to handle even the most difficult obstacles that arise from your beautiful child's ADHD symptoms.

One key factor to always remember is that you are incredibly important to your child; they rely on you for emotional support and mental fortitude. This is why your own self-care is so deeply necessary. Don't forget to pause and give yourself breaks as needed. Sometimes, you won't be able to keep going like a well-oiled machine. Instead, you might need a small break to collect yourself before coming back to your child's needs. There's nothing wrong with scheduling some time to care for your own needs.

By making small changes to yourself, you'll be helping your family dynamic foster healthier communication and praise all of the good behaviors your child makes rather than making them feel bad for their misbehavior. With time and effort, you and your family are on your way to instilling a powerful mindful parenting approach that will keep you all functioning at your very best while keeping the lines of communication open for your child's needs.

You have been given so many tools throughout this book. Now, it's time for you to use them to support and nurture that beautiful child of yours.

References

Book Cover Image: Freepik.com. This cover has been designed using assets from Freepik.com

4 types of communication styles. (2019, April 6). Alvernia University Online. Retrieved October 29, 2021, from https://online.alvernia.edu/articles/4-types-communication-styles/

Alidina, S. (2019, July 17). *Nine ways mindfulness reduces stress*. Mindful. Retrieved October 29, 2021, from https://www.mindful.org/9-ways-mindfulness-reduces-stress/

Anthony, M. (n.d.). *How to foster independence*. Scholastic. Retrieved October 29, 2021, from https://www.scholastic.com/parents/family-life/social-emotional-learning/social-skills-for-kids/how-to-foster-independence.html

Barkley, R. (2021, September 23). *What is an executive function? 7 deficits tied to ADHD*. ADDitude. Retrieved October 29, 2021, from https://www.additudemag.com/7-executive-function-deficits-linked-to-adhd/

Bertin, M. (2021, July 5). *The effects of ADHD on communication.* The A.D.D. Resource Center. Retrieved October 29, 2021, from https://www.addrc.org/effects-adhd-communication/

Bertin, M. (2020, November 17). *How everyday mindfulness can make you a better parent.* ADDitude. Retrieved October 29, 2021, from https://www.additudemag.com/mindful-parenting-adhd-managing-stress/

Bertin, M., Goldstein, E., Ellison, K., Rossy, L., Bullock, B. G., Whitney-Coulter, A., Naidoo, U., & Smookler, E. (2018, October 15). *Mindful parenting for ADHD.* Mindful. Retrieved October 29, 2021, from https://www.mindful.org/mindful-parenting-for-adhd/

Bjarnadottir, A. (2019, June 19). *Mindful eating 101 - A beginner's guide.* Healthline. Retrieved October 29, 2021, from https://www.healthline.com/nutrition/mindful-eating-guide#tips

Calderon, J. (2020, December 16). *Executive function in children:* Why it matters and how to help. Harvard Health. Retrieved October 29, 2021, from https://www.health.harvard.edu/blog/executive-function-in-children-why-it-matters-and-how-to-help-2020121621583

Centers for Disease Control and Prevention. (2021, September 2). *School changes - helping children with ADHD.* Centers for Disease Control and Prevention. Retrieved October 29, 2021, from https://www.cdc.gov/ncbddd/adhd/features/adhd-and-school-changes.html

Davis, T. (n.d.). *Self-care: 12 ways to take better care of yourself.* Psychology Today. Retrieved October 29, 2021, from https://www.psychologytoday.com/us/blog/click-here-happiness/201812/self-care-12-ways-take-better-care-yourself

Decluttering your mind and space with mindfulness. (2020, March 11). eMindful. Retrieved October 29, 2021, from https://emindful.com/2020/03/11/decluttering-with-mindfulness/

Diagnosing ADHD. CHADD. (2020, October 6). CHADD. Retrieved October 29, 2021, from https://chadd.org/about-adhd/diagnosing-adhd/

Emotional health is more important than grades. (2020, October 12). Reach Out Recovery. Retrieved October 29, 2021, from https://reachoutrecovery.com/your-childs-mental-health-is-more-important-than-grades/

Ensroth, K. (n.d.). *Ask an expert: Should I put my child on ADHD medication?* Providence Health & Services, Oregon and Southwest Washington. Retrieved October 29, 2021, from https://oregon.providence.org/forms-and-information/a/ask-an-expert-should-i-put-my-child-on-adhd-medication/

Evaluating childhood ADHD. (2020, September 21). CHADD. Retrieved October 29, 2021, from https://chadd.org/for-parents/evaluating-for-childhood-adhd_qf/

Focus more to ease stress. (2011, December 6). Harvard Health. Retrieved October 29, 2021, from https://www.health.harvard.edu/healthbeat/focus-more-to-ease-stress

Goldstein, E. (2019, February 26). *Stressing out?* S.T.O.P. Mindful. Retrieved October 29, 2021, from https://www.mindful.org/stressing-out-stop/

Glowiak, M. (2020, April 14). *What is self-care and why is it important for you?* Southern New Hampshire University. Retrieved October 29, 2021, from https://www.snhu.edu/about-us/newsroom/health/what-is-self-care

Harpin, V. A. (2005, February 1). *The effect of ADHD on the life of an individual, their family, and community from preschool to adult life.* Archives of Disease in Childhood. Retrieved October 29, 2021, from https://adc.bmj.com/content/90/suppl_1/i2

Hasan, S. (Ed.). (2020, June). *Parenting a child with ADHD (for parents) - nemours kidshealth. KidsHealth.* Retrieved October 29, 2021, from https://kidshealth.org/en/parents/parenting-kid-adhd.html

How to help your child with ADHD complete tasks. (n.d.). Brain Balance Achievement Centers. Retrieved October 29, 2021, from https://www.brainbalancecenters.com/blog/how-to-help-your-child-with-adhd-complete-tasks

How to succeed in high school with ADHD: A teen's guide. (2021, July 29). ADDitude. Retrieved October 29, 2021, from https://www.additudemag.com/high-school-success-adhd-students-homework-studying/

Low, K. (2020, January 7). H*ow to set up a reward system for improving your child's ADHD behavior.* Verywell Mind. Retrieved October 29, 2021, from https://www.verywellmind.com/behavior-management-for-adhd-20867

Low, K. (2020, September 27). *What are the effects of impaired executive functions?* Verywell Mind. Retrieved October 29, 2021, from https://www.verywellmind.com/what-are-executive-functions-20463

Low, K. (n.d.). *Understand what it's like for children with ADHD.* Verywell Mind. Retrieved October 29, 2021, from https://www.verywellmind.com/understanding-children-with-adhd-20686#effects-of-adhd-in-kids

Common misconceptions about ADHD medications. (2019, March 11). Millennium Medical Associates - Adult ADHD Treatment in Los Angeles. Retrieved October 29, 2021, from https://www.millenniummedicalassociates.com/blog/2019/3/11/common-misconceptions-about-adhd-medications

Mindful breathing. (n.d.). Greater Good in Action. Retrieved October 29, 2021, from https://ggia.berkeley.edu/practice/mindful_breathing

Mindful parenting: ADHD and Communication. (2018, July 20). CHADD. Retrieved October 29, 2021, from https://chadd.org/attention-article/mindful-parenting-adhd-and-communication/

Morin, A. (2019, October 22). *How to know if you're a perfectionist parent and what to do about it.* Verywell Family. Retrieved October 29, 2021, from https://www.verywellfamily.com/what-to-know-about-perfectionist-parenting-4163102

Morin, A. (2021, July 2). *How cognitive reframing works.* Verywell Mind. Retrieved October 29, 2021, from https://www.verywellmind.com/reframing-defined-2610419

Attention deficit hyperactivity disorder (ADHD). (n.d.). NHS. Retrieved October 29, 2021, from https://www.nhs.uk/conditions/attention-deficit-hyperactivity-disorder-adhd/symptoms/

Orenstein, B. W. (n.d.). *Managing ADHD when routines change - ADHD and your child.* Everyday Health. Retrieved October 29, 2021, from https://www.everydayhealth.com/hs/adhd-and-your-child/managing-adhd-when-routines-change/

Pace, K. (2018, September 20). *Your mindfulness practice can be formal or informal.* MSU Extension. Retrieved October 29, 2021, from https://www.canr.msu.edu/news/your_mindfulness_practice_can_be_formal_or_informal

Rawe, J. (2021, January 28). *ADHD and the brain.* Understood. Retrieved October 29, 2021, from https://www.understood.org/articles/en/adhd-and-the-brain

Scaccia, A. (2020, August 26). *Depression and vitamin D deficiency.* Healthline. Retrieved October 29, 2021, from https://www.healthline.com/health/depression-and-vitamin-d

Selva, J. (2021, June 21). *History of mindfulness: From east to west and religion to science.* Positive Psychology. Retrieved October 29, 2021, from https://positivepsychology.com/history-of-mindfulness/

Storebø, O. J., Krogh, H. B., Ramstad, E., Moreira-Maia, C. R., Holmskov, M., Skoog, M., Nilausen, T. D., Magnusson, F. L., Zwi, M., Gillies, D., Rosendal, S., Groth, C., Rasmussen, K. B., Gauci, D., Kirubakaran, R., Forsbøl, B., Simonsen, E., & Gluud, C. (2015, November 25). *Methylphenidate for attention-deficit/hyperactivity disorder in children and adolescents: Cochrane systematic review with Meta-analyses and trial sequential analyses of randomised clinical trials.* The BMJ. Retrieved October 29, 2021, from https://www.bmj.com/content/351/bmj.h5203

Studies link ADHD and communication problems. (n.d.). Brain Balance Achievement Centers. Retrieved October 29, 2021, from https://www.brainbalancecenters.com/blog/adhd-and-communication-problems

Tuckman, A. (2021, September 6). *Why is an ADHD diagnosis so important?* ADDitude. Retrieved October 29, 2021, from https://www.additudemag.com/why-is-an-adhd-diagnosis-so-important/

Ricardo, C. (2019, October 24). *The two wings of the bird; mindfulness and self compassion.* A Caring Counselor. Retrieved October 29, 2021, from https://acaringcounselor.com/the-two-wings-of-the-bird-mindfulness-and-self-compassion/

Large-scale MRI study confirms ADHD brain differences. (2020, October 22). Understood. Retrieved October 29, 2021, from https://www.understood.org/articles/en/large-scale-mri-study-confirms-adhd-brain-differences?_sp=87ea7a1f-e259-4124-a609-cc90ede2d4cd.1634059451756

Does ADHD raise the risk of mental health issues? (2021, April 19). Understood. Retrieved October 29, 2021, from https://www.understood.org/articles/en/does-adhd-raise-risk-mental-health-issues

Why you need to make time for self-care. (n.d.). Retrieved October 29, 2021, from https://selecthealth.org/blog/2019/05/why-you-need-to-make-time-for-self-care

Wiener, J. (2020, September 4). *The ripple effect of ADHD in adolescents: Self-perceptions and social relationships.* SAGE Journals. Retrieved October 29, 2021, from https://journals.sagepub.com/doi/abs/10.1177/0829573520936456?journalCode=cjsa

Williams, P., & ADDitude Editors. (2021, May 27). *ADHD in children: Symptoms, evaluations & treatments. ADDitude.* Retrieved October 29, 2021, from https://www.additudemag.com/adhd-in-children-symptoms-diagnosis-treatment/

Williamson, J. (2021, February 16). *Self-talk when you can't control other people: 18 affirmations to keep you moving forward.* Healing Brave. Retrieved October 29, 2021, from https://healingbrave.com/blogs/all/self-talk-when-you-cant-control-other-people

Your day is getting better - starting now. (2021, March 24). ADDitude. Retrieved October 29, 2021, from https://www.additudemag.com/slideshows/adhd-famous-quotes-for-a-bad-day/

www.ingramcontent.com/pod-product-compliance
Lightning Source LLC
Chambersburg PA
CBHW070122110526
44587CB00017BA/3239